Journey
to the Interior

American Versions of Haibun

Edited by Bruce Ross

Charles E. Tuttle Co., Inc.
Boston — Rutland, Vermont — Tokyo

First published in 1998 by Tuttle Publishing, an imprint of Periplus Editions (HK) Ltd., with editorial offices at 153 Milk Street, Boston, Massachusetts 02109.

Cover and interior design: Vernon Press, Inc., Boston.

Cover painting: Asher Brown Durand, *Kindred Spirits*, 1849. The Collection of the New York Public Library Astor, Lenox and Tilden Foundations. It depicts William Cullen Bryant (1794–1878), nature poet and editor, and Thomas Cole (1801–48), leader of the Hudson River school of landscape painting.

Library of Congress Cataloging-in-Publication Data

Journey to the interior : American versions of haibun / edited by Bruce Ross.
    p. cm.
    Includes index.
    ISBN 0-8048-3159-9 (pbk.)
    1. American literature—20th century. 2. American literature—
Japanese influences. 3. Autobiographies—United States.
    4. Haibun, American. 5. Haiku, American. I. Ross, Bruce, 1945–

PS535.J68 1998
811'.5408—dc21   98-10476
                                                     CIP

Distributed by

USA	Japan	Southeast Asia
Charles E. Tuttle Co., Inc.	Tuttle Shokai Ltd.	Berkeley Books Pte. Ltd.
RR 1 Box 231-5	1-21-13, Seki	5 Little Road #08-01
North Clarendon, VT 05759	Tama-ku, Kawasaki-shi	Singapore 536983
Tel.: (802) 773-8930	Kanagawa-ken 214, Japan	Tel.: (65) 280-3320
Tel.: (800) 526-2778	Tel.: (044) 833-0225	Fax.: (65) 280-6290
Fax.: (802) 773-6993	Fax.: (044) 822-0413	

First edition
05 04 03 02 01   00 99 98 97   1 3 5 7 9 10 8 6 4 2
Cover and text design: Vernon Press, Inc., Boston, Massachusetts
Printed in the United States of America

To Astrid Calypso Miriam Andreescu

Contents

A Note on the Haibun   11

Introduction   13

Tom Clausen
    Before School   87
    Birds   88
    New Sneakers   90

Jean Dubois
    The Near and Far   91

Charles H. Easter
    Turtle   93

Judson Evans
    Haibun for Dennis: December 12, 1994   95
    The Red   96

Patrick Frank
    Return to Springfield: Urban Haibun   97

Penny Harter
    At Home   100
    A Weekend at Dai Bosatsu Zendō   102

Jim Kacian
    Bright All   111
    The Order of Stars   114

Dennis Kalkbrenner
    Lake Superior   116

Adele Kenny

    Only a Stranger   117

Michael Ketchek

    Chaco Canyon Haibun   120

George Klacsanzky

    Arriving with the Tide   121
    The Black Forest   133

Leatrice Lifshitz

    Far from Home   138

D. S. Lliteras

    Idiot   141
    Zazen   142

Tom Lynch

    Climbing Kachina Peaks   143
    Even as We Sleep   148
    Rain Drips from the Trees   148

Patricia Neubauer

    The Goldfish Vendor   165

H. F. Noyes

    Pines   166

Brent Partridge

    Road Through the Stars: Feb. 24–27, 1994   168

Anthony J. Pupello

    St. Mark's Place   172

William M. Ramsey

    Gurdjieff, Zen, and Meher Baba   174
    Prayer for the Soul of a Mare   177

Bruce Ross

      Aglow   180

      Winter Moon   181

Hal Roth

      Winter Haibun   182

G. R. Simser

      Water Spider   183

Robert Spiess

      A Mosquito Net on Tobago   184

Dave Sutter

      Italia: Quattrocento/Ventecento   190

Tom Tico

      Reaching for the Rain   195

J. P. Trammell

      Sunset on Cadillac Mountain   200

      The Temple of the Snail   201

Frank Trotman

      Early Morning   204

Cor van den Heuvel

      The Circus   205

      Curbstones   209

Rich Youmans

      For My Wife on Our First Anniversary   212

      Sunday Visits   212

      Bibliography   215

      Permissions   217

      Index of Poets   220

A Note on the Haibun

The title of this collection alludes to the well-known seventeenth-century travel journal by Matsuo Bashō, *Oku-no-hosomichi*, which might be freely translated as *Narrow Path to the Interior*. In his old age Bashō, who may be credited with establishing the haiku form, undertook a long journey to the remote regions of northern Japan, fully expecting to die before completing it. He did complete the journey, and his record of it has become a classic of world literature and an example, in its broadest sense, of *haibun*, autobiographical poetic prose accompanied by haiku.

American versions of the form began to appear in the late fifties with travel diaries by Gary Snyder and fiction by Jack Kerouac. In the late sixties work identified as haibun was published in American haiku journals. From the seventies through the nineties the typical form was a one-paragraph nature sketch that ended in a haiku. However, there has been also a wealth of experimentation in form, with book-length travel journals, many-sectioned autobiographical accounts, and experimental fiction, and in subject matter, with erotic self-revelations, social commentaries, historical re-creations, and the like. These directions have produced such deft contemporary practitioners of the form as Jim Kacian, Tom Lynch, and William M. Ramsey. But in many ways the title of this collection is justified in its depiction of the decidedly American way that this conservative Japanese form has been transformed to serve a poetic exploration of the unfathomable interior of the self, the emotional nature of love for another, the deep structure of aesthetic value in nonhuman nature, the implicative sense of dwelling in a particular place, the profound revelation of the unknown place, the hidden well-springs of our spiritual sense—all in the context of the so-called late twentieth-century postmodern condition. Although space and aesthetic constraints prevent the inclusion of many haibun discussed in the Introduction, all such creative overtures are invaluable at this stage of the development of this new American form. Similarly, many of the strong haibun reprinted in the anthology, though not discussed in the Introduction, speak for themselves. Readers interested in exploring haibun further should consult the bibliography. The authors of the haibun collected for this volume are to be congratulated for such eventful explorations and for forging an important addition to American literature.

Introduction

There is not great distance between Bashō's banana hut and Thoreau's cabin at Walden Pond, nor Bashō's *Oku-no-hosomichi* (Narrow Path to the Interior, 1694) and Thoreau's *A Week on the Concord and Merrimack Rivers* (1849) and *The Maine Woods* (1864). In fact, modern versions of North American haibun, a form perfected in Bashō's classic work, allude to Thoreau and his example at Walden Pond more than to any other literary figure. In a variety of stylistic approaches, North American haibun is evolving toward the spiritual depth evoked by both the Japanese master and our own iconoclast naturalist.

Yet there is a presiding disjunction between the aesthetic premises underlying the literary writing, particularly of nature, in the long history of Eastern culture and the fairly short history of American literary writing from the Puritans to the present. One aspect of this disjunction is the manner in which each accounts for the relation of consciousness to external nature.

Broadly speaking, the poetics of the East reflects an ontological union of man's consciousness with nature in which nature is of equal valence to man while the poetics of the West reflects an allegorical subsuming of nature in which man dominates nature. Eastern and Western concepts of subjectivity thus differ, the East accenting an emotional relation of the self to nature and the West accenting an intellectual relation to nature. In the East nature tends to dominate consciousness. In the West the mind tends to determine consciousness.[1]

This Eastern impetus toward universal subjectivity, which would elicit our poetic empathies for nature in its myriad identities, is subverted in America at the first by our inheritance of simple Christian allegory and later by the predominating mechanisms of materialism, science, and philosophic naturalism. In this condition American poetry, especially contemporary poetry, would reflect an inability to treat the ontological realities of nature with sympathy.[2] However, there have been influential waves of the direct influence of Eastern aesthetics upon such American writers as Ralph Waldo Emerson, Henry David Thoreau, Walt Whitman, Ezra Pound, T. S. Eliot, Kenneth Rexroth, Jack Kerouac, Gary Snyder, and Allen Ginsberg. A literary form in which most of these writers could—in the broadest sense—be said to be writing is the Japanese haibun.

A simple definition of the form, taken from a contemporary Japanese-English dictionary, is a "terse prose-poem."[3] Yet this definition does not account for the eliding of the haibun into similar traditional Japanese forms like the *kiko* ("travel journal") and the *nikki* ("diary"). This confluence is addressed in a definition of haibun in a scholarly encyclopedia of Japanese literature: "*Haikai* (related to *renga* composition and sometimes the seventeen-syllable opening verse of a *renga*) writing. Prose composition, usually with haikai stanzas, by a haikai poet. Normally with an autobiographical or theoretical interest, it could treat many kinds of experiences. When it treats a journey, it becomes a species of *kiko*."[4]

The important distinctions in the broader definition of the haibun are that it is autobiographical prose, usually accompanied by verse. Bashō in fact assigned the phrase *michi no nikki* ("diary of the road") to haibun-like travel journals like his *Oku-no-hosomichi*. The deciding factors in considering a literary diary a haibun are that its prose is poetical and that it contains verse, usually haiku. A more recent example is in the work of the first important modern haiku poet, Masaoka Shiki (1867–1902), who published diaries that included sequences of haiku and *tanka*. The usual forms of Japanese haibun up to the modern period were a short sketch of a person, place, event, or object; a travel diary like Bashō's *Narrow Path to the Interior*; or a diary of events in one's life like Kobayashi Issa's (1763–1827) *Oraga Haru* (My Spring, 1819).

Definitions of haibun by scholars of Japanese literature are broad enough to incorporate all the directions that English-language haibun has taken.[5] Further, although the Haiku Society of America—the largest society devoted to haiku and related forms outside Japan—did not include haibun in its official definitions of Japanese forms at first (1973), by 1994 haibun had become a familiar enough form to warrant an official definition:

A short prose essay in the humorous haikai style, usually including a haiku, often at the end. "Haibun" is sometimes applied to the more serious diary or journal writing typical of Bashō's and Issa's longer works, though technically they are part of the diary or journal literature, which is usually more serious than haibun. But it is not unusual for haikai elements to enter into these longer works.[6]

Notwithstanding this comprehensive definition, the actual practice of modern shorter haibun in English includes, as we shall see, serious as well as lighter treatments of given subjects.

Versions of haibun in English first began to appear in Eric Amann's journal *Haiku* (1967–1976).[7] By 1993 three of the more prominent American haiku journals, *Frogpond*, *Modern Haiku*, and *Brussels Sprout*, and one new journal, *Point Judith Light*, had identified poetry and prose entries as haibun. Patrick Frank, the editor of *Point Judith Light*, also offered a short definition at the top of his journal's haibun column: "Haiku embedded within a relatively short prose piece."[8] This definition accurately reflects what is commonly published as haibun in the American haiku journals, with some interesting exceptions, as would be

the case given the space limitations of such journals. But American haibun more properly began with published diaries and haibun-like fiction.

The American literary tradition prepared our early haibun writers with major examples of autobiographical and biographical narrative
that evoked episodes of spiritual challenge or revelation in relation to the
natural world, as well as to social conditions. The more obvious examples
include William Bradford's (1590–1657) historical account *History of
Plymouth Plantation, 1620–1647*, Jonathan Edwards's (1703–1758)
"Personal Narrative" (c. 1740), Benjamin Franklin's (1706–1790) *The
Autobiography* (1867), Henry David Thoreau's (1817–1862) naturalist's
journal *Walden* (1854), and, though poetry, Walt Whitman's (1819–1892)
response to the Civil War, *Drum Taps* (1865). Of these only *Walden*
evokes the Eastern tradition of the spiritual recluse, as Thoreau's travel
writing evokes the Eastern tradition of poetic pilgrimage, both of which
are exemplified in the poetry and travel journals of the Japanese poets
Saigyō (1118–1190) and Sōgi (1421–1502), who had influenced Bashō's
own travel journals. A transitional American writer leading to English-
language haibun is the naturalist John Muir (1838–1914), through his
prose accounts and diaries of his travels in the American wilderness, such
as *The Mountains of California* (1894) and *John of the Mountains* (1938).

The so-called Beat Movement of the 1950s reflects the second
major influx of Eastern thought and literary conventions, after the
Transcendentalists, into American history. This group, under the nomi-
nal tutelage of Kenneth Rexroth—naturalist, landscape poet, and trans-
lator of Chinese and Japanese poetry—attempted to model their lives on
the lives of the Eastern recluse and pilgrimage poets, in spite of their
confirmed adherence to seemingly non-Eastern passionately indulgent
experience. The seminal, and perhaps earliest, work of this group that
approaches the haibun in tone and structure is Gary Snyder's *Earth
House Hold* (1957), a collection of work journals, travel diaries, reviews,

translations, biographical accounts, and essays whose central focus is Zen Buddhism. Snyder studied Zen in Japan for a number of years and includes in the collection a journal of his first travel to and religious study in Japan, as well as an account of an intensive meditation retreat at a Zen monastery in Kyoto. But it is his "Lookout's Journal," a poetic log of his work as a fire spotter in the mountains of Washington State, that offers a model of what American haibun was to become.

The entry for August 6, 1952, serves as an example of how elements from the classical Japanese haibun, consciously or not, incorporated themselves into the stream of American literary journals:

Clouds above and below, but I can see Kulshan, Mt. Terror Shuksan; they blow over the ridge between here and Three-fingered Jack, fill up the valleys. The Buckner Boston Peak ridge is clear.

What happens all winter; the wind driving snow; clouds— wind, and mountains—repeating

this is what always happens here

and the photograph of a young female torso hung in the lookout window, in the foreground. Natural against natural, beauty.

two butterflies
a chilly clump of mountain
flower

zazen   non-life. An art: mountain-watching.

leaning in the doorway whistling
a chipmunk popped out
listening[9]

This selection manifests the four characteristics that Makoto Ueda attributes to haibun in his discussion of Bashō's prose: (1) "a brevity and conciseness of haiku," (2) "a deliberately ambiguous use of certain particles and verb forms in places where the conjunction 'and' would be used in English," (3) a "dependence on imagery," and (4) "the writer's detachment."[10] The entry, like many of the others in "Lookout's Journal"—though a bit more radically spaced on the page than the typical prose of *Earth House Hold*—intersperses short prose passages with haiku-like poems. Although Snyder may not have been intentionally writing haibun, he was clearly writing haiku in the context of classical haiku aesthetics: in one section he notes that he had written "a haiku and painted a *haiga* for it" and in another he discusses the concept of *sabi*, which is at the heart of Bashō's mature conception of haiku.[11] And, as in this entry, poems that clearly look and sound like haiku appear. Both of the haiku in this entry, like traditional haiku, are made of juxtaposed images succinctly expressed and allude, directly or indirectly, to a given season: in the first, summer butterflies are connected with the stationary mountain flowers they investigate; in the second, Snyder whistling in the doorway is connected to the (summer) chipmunk that listens to him. Further, the deep resonance built up in the first around the word "chilly" and the in-the-moment humor of the second that is underscored by the rhyming of "whistling" and "listening" make these good haiku.

The prose itself maintains the haiku values that Ueda finds in haibun. Except when Snyder directly cites conversation, the prose entries are expressed in a pared-down, often telegraphic, syntax that is dominated by images, often to the point of Zen-like cosmic simplicity, as in this line from the entry under discussion: "*zazen*   non-life.   An art: mountain-watching." The evident Zennian mood expresses the ego-detachment which is Ueda's fourth characteristic of haibun. Thus, "Lookout's Journal" provides a paradigm, however rarefied, for American haibun: a short poetic autobiographical narrative that includes haiku.

Jack Kerouac, the chronicler of the Beat Generation, immortalized Snyder as the character Japhy Ryder in the novel *The Dharma Bums* (1958), a novelistic account of that generation's attempts to achieve Buddhist enlightenment through retreats like the one described in Snyder's "Lookout's Journal." In one episode of Kerouac's novel Japhy offers a homespun definition of haiku: "A real haiku's gotta be as simple as porridge and yet make you see the real thing...."[12] Here the Zennian interest in correctly aligning one's consciousness with reality supports Japhy's Bashō-like insistence on the objective presentation of images, of the ontologic value of those images, in haiku. This value of "the real thing" also determines the mood of what is best in American haibun: engaging our narrated experience (and critical appreciations) to their spiritual depths.

The classic Japanese novel *The Tale of Genji* (c. 1000), by Marasaki Shikibu, provides a model for including poetry (here *tanka*) in a fictional narrative. The direction culminates in the fiction of Natsume Soseki (1867–1916), such as in his *Kasamakura* (The Three-Cornered World, 1906), which intersperses haiku and discussions about haiku in its first-person poetic narrative fiction. The published diaries of Masaoka Shiki, with their inclusion of haiku and tanka sequences, offer a bridge between the autobiographical poetic journals of Snyder and the fictionalized autobiography of Kerouac.

Jack Kerouac's long novel *Desolation Angels* (1965) again narrates the search for spiritual awakening. Perhaps because haiku are testimonies to moments of such awakening, the chapters of "Book One" of the novel often culminate in one or two haiku. But whereas the haiku in

Snyder's "Lookout's Journal" convey the lucidity of a consciousness perceiving reality calmly from an awakened state, so that these images have a Bashō-like objective depth, as in his haiku on a drowned mouse found in his morning water bucket,[13] making such haiku one more account in a day's events, the haiku in *Desolation Angels* crystallize in an almost discursive way a moment of personal realization precipitated by the given prose narrative. In such narrative, expressed by Kerouac in poetically compressed, rhythmic prose chapters of about one to three paragraphs, we find represented, more than in Snyder, albeit in a more comprehensively subjective way, the stylistic mode of typical American haibun in which haiku more or less complete given straightforward narrative development.

For example, in chapter forty-one of *Desolation Angels*, the novel's narrator and main character sleeps on Desolation Peak, the site of his fire-watching job, as the rainy season begins. This one-paragraph chapter is introduced by a short comment on the rain, but for most of its length describes a dream of the narrator and his thoughts and memories in response to that dream. The chapter's narration concludes with a quotation from the Buddha on dreams and the true nature of reality. The two haiku appended to this chapter recapitulate all of the elements of the narrative, but, further, offer a moment of revelation derived from it.[14] The first haiku leads from an image of the rain ("mist boiling") to an insight into the true nature of the surrounding mountains (they are "clean" in the rain) in the Buddhist context of the universality of subjectivity in which all things have their own consciousness and exist "just as they are." The second haiku leads from another image of the rain ("mist"), through the narrator's dream (which "goes on"), to the implicative contradictory Buddhist ideas of the illusory nature of reality (*samsara*) and the cosmic nature of this same reality when perceived in an awakened state (*nirvana*).

Another chapter from the novel is a character study of a colorful old Glacier District ranger who is described to the narrator by a character named Jarry Wagner, another stand-in for Gary Snyder. The ranger comments on Jarry: "'And all dem books he reads...about Buddha and all dat, he's the smart one all right dat Jarry.'"[15] This affectionate account by the old ranger is ironically juxtaposed by the narrator to Jarry's actual Buddhist practice. And at the thought of Jarry meditating across the ocean in Japan, the narrator is provoked to the realization that "Buddha's just as old and true anywhere you go...."[16] This opposition leads to the chapter's concluding melding of the old ranger with Buddhism and, in the light of the ranger's weather-beaten, unmarried, isolated state, with the mountain and its buddha-nature in a haiku that asks the mountain, Desolation Peak, how it "earned" its name.[17]

In a final example, another chapter recounts the narrator's departure from the mountain at the end of his tour of duty. After offering a prayer to his cabin, he meditates upon the beauty and cosmic mystery of a lake in the far distance. He then acknowledges his love of God for creating such beauty and mystery as evoked by the lake. This testament precipitates a final awareness which will prepare the narrator for his reentry into the world of men: "Whatever happens to me down that trail to the world is all right with me because I am God and I'm doing it all myself, who else?"[18] He realizes that, in Buddhist terms, there is no theistic God, there is no ordinary self, only buddha-nature, which is a correct orientation of consciousness, and that he is responsible for achieving that consciousness. The concluding haiku, which explains the narrator's ability to accomplish this state through meditation, such as in his contemplation of the lake, declares, "I am Buddha," and thus becomes a recorded moment of such a state.[19]

Experiments with longer versions of haibun in the seventies and early eighties include Geraldine Little's *Separation: Seasons in Space:*

A Western Haibun (1979) and Hal Roth's *Behind the Fireflies* (1982). The latter offers prose accounts of an American Civil War battle by Roth as well as by eye-witnesses, whose writings are juxtaposed to Roth's contemporary haiku.

An ambitious work that unites the narrative drive of traditional modern fiction and the emotional power of haiku appended to poetic prose in haibun is Rod Willmot's *Ribs of Dragonfly* (1984). Each of the work's nine sections begins with a short prose "Prelude" on the narrator's stormy year-long relationship with a woman named Leila. Each "Prelude" is then followed by a number of impressionistic narrative prose sketches that evoke either the narrator's experiences while canoeing in nature over the course of three seasons or his problematic relationship with Leila. Finally, each section closes with a group of haiku, from eight to nineteen in number, some relating directly to the prose sketches.

Canadian haiku poet Willmot edited the anthology *Erotic Haiku* (1983), and *Ribs of Dragonfly* propels itself in part from the erotic drive of the narrator's relation with Leila, whose name links her to Eastern concepts of illusion. That drive is manifested in the longing of this haiku:

> bathing, I think of you
> and lift the straw blind
> to the rain[20]

The narrative theme of adultery that supports this drive is evoked compellingly in the following:

> lying beside you
> thinking of her hair
> all night the cries of gulls[21]

Though the narrative of the relationship is at times overdrawn and melo-dramatic, the power of these and similarly erotic haiku carry half the haibun, beginning with the first of such haiku, which occurs in the group appended to the work's first section:

> she hugs me from behind
> my face in the steam
> of the potatoes[22]

The other half of the haibun is carried by the impressionistic prose sketches of nature, which will prompt the narrator to an exploration of the nature of consciousness, such as this from the first section:

Silence.

On the horizon, drab sketches in olive and sepia of conifers and cottage woodlots. Ice-huts here and there, too distant for motion to be discerned among them or in their tiny plumes of smoke. The ice impassive now, no longer apprenticed to the rhythms of cold as when it boomed and sang responsively. Master of silence in its death. The water, at times wholly reflection, at times pure darkness, at times more silvery than ice. And over everything, the shroud.

Stillness, even in me: a void between each breath where I linger heedlessly, accepting. Yet movement. A fragrance melting. Movement I could smell.[23]

The perceptual silence and stillness of the passage, a prologue to an engagement with a Zen-like consciousness in the work, is echoed in this haiku from the same section:

mail on the counter

sits unopened

afternoon sun through birches[24]

This consciousness, which in Willmot is usually linked with sensu-
ousness, reaches a synthesis of sorts through the psychological dialectic of subjectivity and objectivity described in a late section of the
work:

I have felt foreign to the world, honoring its mask of oneness and
certitude. But now I see that it is me, or my portrait, endlessly
shifting as I do. My infinite anatomy. Then am I so miserable as I
seem? Everything I've seen or touched has been a sketch of my
insides. That field of rotting cabbages in snow, malodorous, but
with a dance of pheasant-tracks stitched among the rows, ele-
gant and clean. Those crystal "berries" in a chunk of porphyry,
rock within rock and unpluckable, until I tossed it into a pond
and received, startled, the resonant fruit of sound. And the
mossy woods along the coast where we searched all morning for
the source of a strange perfume, until its very hiddenness
became a kind of mushroom, edible, that grew within our heads.

Which of us maps the other, World?
Birch-leaves, trembling as I watch them.[25]

The enigmatic nature of this synthesis of inner and outer reality that is
held in Zen-like stillness while yet being presidingly sensuous is movingly exhibited in one of the haiku following this passage:

amid the wild rice
chewing
the bittern's stillness[26]

But for all the monumental depth of its exploration of such consciousness, *Ribs of Dragonfly* is still explorative, if sentimental, fiction, and,
unlike the haiku in *Desolation Angels* and almost all American haibun, its
appended haiku for the most part relate to the general mood of the work
as a whole and not to the specific section to which they are appended.

Another ambitious chapbook-length haibun is Vincent Tripi's
Haiku Pond: A trace of the trail...and Thoreau (1987). The work, all of whose
profits go to the Thoreau Society, represents an act of spiritual communion
with Thoreau and his vision as expressed in *Walden*. The work consists of
Tripi's journal entries and haiku relating to Walden Pond, Thoreau's spirit,
and present-tense nature from the spring of 1984 to the autumn of 1985.
Thus the work adheres to Thoreau's temporal structure for *Walden*,
although Tripi's journal entries are not in chronological order. This material is interspersed with quotations from Thoreau and sumi-like paintings.
Tripi conceives of each page as producing a haiku-like aesthetic whole. As
he notes in his Introduction: "Each page becomes a 'picture'—the pond
'infinity,' the symbols 'life,' and the poems and art 'the spark' that makes
them one."[27] The connection of the given page to the "haiku moment" is
then made explicit: "The 'pictures' when settled are themselves moment-to-
moment awakenings of mind...a passing of water in the night."[28]

The communion with Thoreau is introduced in the first entry of
the first of the four sections of *Haiku Pond*. On this page Tripi creates his
imagined invitation to communion by quoting from Thoreau's *Journal*: "I
should be pleased to meet a man in the woods. I wish he were encoun-

tered like wild caribous and moose."[29] Tripi responds as that man with an
entry from his own journal: "Solitude was the face in whose smile…my
eyes began to find themselves again."[30] The source of that solitude, the
experiment recorded in *Walden*, is illustrated on the next page with a
drawing of Walden Pond. The following page continues this dialogue with
an entry from Thoreau on solitude, followed by a haiku and journal entry
by Tripi, which consider Thoreau's and Tripi's own relation to Walden
Pond as a focus for meditation and higher consciousness in nature.

This consciousness is firmly established for Tripi in the second
section. One page from this section inserts this haiku between quotations from Thoreau's *Journal* on the visual clarity of nature at sunset and
on guarding one's spiritual purity:

White moon,
Snowman's shadow
Gone.[31]

Tripi, like the snowman without a shadow, has attained a purity of spirit
that is selflessly united with nature. The haiku is followed by Tripi's journal
entry, which is a haibun, entitled "The Way of Spruce," that exhibits this
purity of consciousness that fuses itself completely with external nature:

The way of spruce begins to glisten. Sleeper in
things, the green-wet woodsmoke disappears.
It is enough to fill myself with clouds. A speckled
alder, a broken willow…from the bottom.

Woodsmoke—
Dusk
In the grass-spider's web.[32]

In the second paragraph of the haibun Tripi's consciousness seems to become Walden Pond itself, reflecting the clouds and containing the sunken trees. The concluding haiku intensifies the haibun's concern with manifesting a clarity of consciousness that will selflessly reflect the objective realities of nature in their cloud-like continuous becomings by objectively focusing on such realities in a moment at dusk. That concern had been already introduced, almost as an epigraph, in Thoreau's journal entry at the top of the same page: at sunset, he notes, "ponds are white and distinct."[33] The radical complexity and compressed nature of the reverberations built up among the images on this page are typical of *Haiku Pond*, which, as a work, provides the most experimental use of images thus far in English-language haibun.

The moodiness and *sabi*-like feeling of the concluding haiku are set within the context of actual meditation practice two pages later in the haibun "Scarecrow." This haibun records the objective sense perceptions of the meditator's heightened awareness of silence. It also evokes the central tenet of Buddhism, the inevitable dissolution of human consciousness and all things in death, through the symbolic image of wind: "Wind-within. It sits with me...the scarecrow on the hill."[34] This passage is followed by a drawing of Tripi in the lotus meditation position. Tripi himself thus becomes the human scarecrow who in as objective a way as possible registers the fact of his mortality as a facet of reality. This haibun's concluding haiku imposes this fact, however gloomy, upon Tripi's communion with Thoreau, whose *Journal* is alluded to in its first line:

> Not his Journal
> But the winter wind
> Is sad.[35]

This *sabi*-like reckoning with mortality, which is, as Tripi notes in this haiku, alien to the Transcendentalist spirit and Thoreau's work, makes

Tripi's *Haiku Pond* all the more compelling as a spiritual journal that is perhaps understood and colored as much by a postmodern despair as it is by a *sabi*-like aesthetic.

But a universal insight into nature that is ecstatic rather than moody, and thus precisely in the spirit of Thoreau, occurs in the last section of *Haiku Pond*. This section begins with the following quote from Thoreau: "Silence is audible to all men, at all times, and in all places."[36] It is followed by Tripi's journal entry on silence. The silence here is intended to be the same kind of Zennian objectivity before all experience that we have already discussed. The next page confirms this intent with a drawing of a splash which, as we learn in the next page's haiku, wittily alludes to Bashō's most famous haiku:

> This morning from a frog,
> I hear all I need to hear—
> About the pond![37]

So in silence, a state of enlightened consciousness, Tripi commingles Bashō's frog pond with Thoreau's Walden Pond. He highlights further this intent by having Thoreau speak like a haiku poet: "My profession is to be always on the alert to find God in nature..."[38] If we substitute "objective revelation" for "God," we have brought Thoreau and Bashō together. And then immediately Tripi has the last word by joyfully linking, in a subtle manner, his cabin, Thoreau's cabin at Walden Pond, and, possibly, Bashō's hut, to the tone and structure of Bashō's frog haiku:

> Cabin door
> POP!
> In July.[39]

Thus Tripi has united, in this haiku and *Haiku Pond* as a whole, the spiritual visions of Bashō and Thoreau, the Eastern communion with nature that is echoed in American Transcendentalism.

Ralph Waldo Emerson, the leader of that movement, noticed a "fundamental unity" between man and nature. Here is the American paradigm for the idea of universal subjectivity: all of reality, including non-human nature, has its own inherent reality with its own right to existence. Man may not, at his whim, subjugate that seemingly mindless otherness to his own will. In fact, as Emerson would suggest, there is an inherent beneficent relation between man's consciousness and those non-human subjectivities through which man's inner life is enriched. These are the subjectivities that Thoreau studied and communed with during his stay at Walden Pond. And these are the subjectivities that Bashō advised his students to study and commune with. In sum, haiku and haibun are revelations of such study and communion. One aspect of such a poetics involves the Zennian idea of seeing things just as they are, that is, in their own subjectivity or buddha-nature which, in Zennian terms, reflects a universal subjectivity of consciousness. Another aspect of such a poetics involves the Buddhist value of compassion toward all living things: a broad-based respect for nature, including humanity, that is perhaps expressed in the contemporary ideas surrounding the ecology movement. A final aspect of such a poetics involves the Taoist and Buddhist idea of the ephemeral yet cosmic nature of the moment: that each subjectivity is created and sustained anew moment-to-moment. Hence the mystery of universal creation itself is concealed in a particularized way in each moment experienced, in each subjectivity experienced.

The most common form of English-language haibun consists of one to three fairly short paragraphs followed by a single haiku that sums up or comments on the preceding prose, although a variation of the form intersperses haiku throughout the prose. These prose sections of a haibun are most often expressed in a heightened "poetic" tone that is matched likewise by the accompanying haiku. Such haibun equally represent most often a direct response to some facet of nature. And the majority of the more successful of these address the mystery of universal subjectivity in its moment-to-moment manifestation.

Three examples of such successful haibun are set, appropriately, during the periods of sunrise or sunset when the claims of our ordinary daytime consciousness and so-called objectivity are loosened. Hal Roth's winter haibun and Dennis Kalkbrenner's "Lake Superior" occur at dawn. Both are expressed in a dream-like mood that evokes Chuang-tzu's Taoism with its emphasis on the ephemeral, perhaps illusory, nature of perceived reality. So-called objectivity is broken down by such a mood and the non-human subjectivities are revealed to us. For Roth in a bleak winter field, they are the evoked pathos of a sapling that will die because of wounds created by a buck's rubbing against it and the haunting personified winds, both of which are incorporated into the concluding haiku:

> midwinter—
> dawn winds approach
> the buck's rubbing tree[40]

For Kalkbrenner, skipping stones on Lake Superior in the summer, it is the very recovery of a child-like capacity to commune with those non-human subjectivities. The prose thus concludes: "Awake again all young dreams."[41] And this process, provoked by the fragrance of roses and the misty lake, is concretized in a metaphor of those half-forgotten dreams in the fading echoes of the skipped stones described in the haibun's concluding haiku.

J. P. Trammell's "Sunset on Cadillac Mountain" reverses the oriental convention of watching sunrise from a holy mountain. Here

Trammell's seemingly objective presentation of the perceptual transformations caused by sunset on the mountains to the west and the inhabited islands to the east of Cadillac Mountain comes to elicit a poetically charged response to what Trammell experiences: like whales, "humped islands rise in the bays"; the sun, like a creature, seems to "settle onto the knobs and ridges of the pink and blue mountains"; the waters appear fiery silver "as if poured molten from a ladle."[42] But with darkness a different subjectivity of the mountain is manifested. The lights of the stars and those of the inhabited dwellings on the islands and in the forests surrounding the mountain produce a *sabi*-like mood: "I am alone in the encroaching darkness…" and evoke the *sabi*-mooded objectivity of the concluding haiku in which an unseen yarrow's fragrance "penetrates the night."[43]

G. R. Simser's "Water Spider," in the act of describing the play of that creature's shadow on the bottom of a brook, occasions a startling emotional process that commingles perception, illusion, objectivity, subjectivity, dream, memory, revelation, and spirituality. In a tour de force of compression Simser moves from the breath-like five-part shadow of the creature to an epiphany of material creation itself:

> …five ephemeral pods closing together to become one and then opening and closing again and again, motions in time tracing breath's flow over bony ribs; tracing briefly the crucifix, the magic discovery of *homo ad circulum's* head, hands and feet, and then the snow-angel wonder of youth, arms pumping its wings to exhaustion, then finally fully extended these magic pods become our gliding five-point star; while all the while above us, somewhere, floats the draughtsman, silent and unseen, of such natural art.…[44]

The allusions to God and Christianity in Simser's act of perceptual meditation are clearly evident, the water spider becoming a metaphor of

God's sustaining moment-to-moment creation and, by consequent extension, of the interrelationship of all realities, of, ultimately, universal subjectivity. Such associative complexity leads Simser to the realization that the individual human has many realities within his or her self and the haibun's prose ends with this realization: "...we too continue to float in many dimensions...."[45] The concluding haiku reinforces both this realization and that of universal subjectivity by describing, in a return to the objective creature, the water spider's shadow which, in the haiku's third line, has, like human beings, "many dimensions."[46]

The democratic compassion tacitly expressed in linking man's nature to that of a water spider is straightforwardly presented in Liz Fenn's "No Monkey Business," a simple narrative of the nourishment and release of five orphaned newborn mice that were found in the family's house. The mother in this haibun expresses her love for her son's act of kindness in rescuing the mice but worries that one of the mice will return to be caught in one of the family's seemingly necessary traps. Notwithstanding the apparent lack of awareness of cruelty-free traps, the haibun ends on an upbeat note with a *senryu*-like expression of universal good will in a haiku that notes that a "no trespassing" sign has been placed in the house's crawl space.[47]

Another common form of English-language haibun is the travel journal. The standard for such a form is set by Bashō's *Narrow Path to the Interior*. Besides the artistry with which Bashō commingles deftly descriptive prose narrative and deeply evocative haiku, this work and others like it resonate with a shared cultural history. That history, which includes centuries of poetic responses to well-known natural and cultural settings, augments whatever artistry is present in a given travel journal. But without the artistry, mere reliance on familiar or exotic settings alone cannot carry the work. Robert Spiess, editor of *Modern Haiku*, in a discussion of haiku sequences based on travel, noted that most of such "'vacation haiku'…are too much recordings of stimuli, rather than creative, in-depth work."[48] A great number of published short travel haibun unfortunately support this view. The best of such haibun reckon with the resonances of history upon the modern present felt moment, expressed in haiku, within the context of the given haibun's travel narrative. So, in these works, the haiku carry the narrative. Dave Sutter's "Italia: Quattrocento/Ventecento," as its title indicates, is a light essay on the impingement of the Renaissance and other past Italian history on the decidedly flamboyant present-day modern culture in what Sutter calls a "quintessence of contrasts and extremes."[49] Perhaps generated by Sutter's visit to the cemetery where his uncle, who died as an American serviceman in Europe, is buried, this haibun discusses the observed contrasts in a straightforward manner, almost always exemplifying each of its eleven paragraphs with a forthright illustrative haiku. If you are charmed by the "light touch" of the prose and the haiku, you will enjoy the haibun. But most of its haiku are based on a simple direct contrast that unambiguously underscores the work's thesis: a blind man selling broken statues, farmhouses eight hundred years apart in age, schoolchildren leaning to look at the Tower of Pisa, a topless woman compared to Botticelli's *Birth of Venus*. Unless you feel the aesthetic weight of the thesis, the success of the work's haiku comes from the simple irony of the depicted contrasts.

More successful is J. P. Trammell's "The Temple of the Snail,"[50] an account of a visit to the ruins of the temple of Ixchel, the Mayan moon goddess, on the Mexican Caribbean island of Cozumel. The haibun conveys a poetic entrance into the realm of sacred history as concretized by the temple (Trammell quotes from Wordsworth's *The Prelude* on this theme) and manifested in the seemingly protective barrier of a rainstorm that Trammell must cross in order to commune with the sacredness of the temple. His taking shelter in the temple leads him to a heightened perception of spiritualized time and space, evoked by a colony of hermit crabs that climb out from the temple floor carrying colorful seashells and fossils that rise from the weathered surface of the temple's stonework. Thus the temple and its mystery are somehow animated for the narrator and we are left to make the connections generated in him by these observations.

Leatrice Lifshitz's "Far From Home" is a postmodern meditation on the grounding of the self in history and the space-time coordinates of perceived experience. Its evident theme is gender and exploration. The context of the work is a trip west that mirrors pioneer women's treks across America. The tone is set in this interior monologue in a consideration of what essentially is the reality of space and time:

Space. A woman in space. Finally.

traveling west—
all those wide open spaces
fenced in

Does that mean that space is gone? Used up? Well, if it isn't space, it's space coupled with time. Changed into time. The time to cross a bridge. Back and forth.[51]

The narrator begins by alluding to the first female astronaut and to the vanishing of the American frontier. This leads her to the conception of a new frontier, a dialectic between history and present-tense locality. This dialectic is expressed later in a visit to a cemetery and an abandoned mine. The narrator is trying to make sense of the dialectic but only becomes further disoriented: She is, as she says, "Wandering outside the chain of life."[52] She is now beyond even history and the concrete moment. The concluding haiku conclusively evokes this final state:

> far from home—
> one crow or another
> waking me[53]

This "rhythm of sameness," as she calls it, this postmodern malaise, breaks down the singularity of experience at the heart of haiku and haibun as much as it breaks down the traditionally reliable continuity of history. Most English-language travel haibun, however, takes a confident stance in the basic coordinates of space and time, including historical time, by ranging from the light travelogue to what might be termed spiritual literature.

Fewer than a dozen chapbook-length travel haibun have been published. The majority of these, and the few unpublished chapbook-length travel haibun that I am familiar with, aspire to that latter kind of literature. Perhaps the earliest published modern chapbook-length haibun is Robert Spiess's *Five Caribbean Haibun* (1972), a collection of haibun and accompanying drawings, one of which was published in *Travel* magazine. The work is in the "lighter" mode of conveying felt experience, and its exotic locations resonate with the vibrancy and narrative interest inherent in the given locales, such as the description of a fisherman scrubbing a moray eel and an octopus, his dinner, or an encounter with poisonous cave spiders. Some of the prose and haiku is a bit too light in tone and focus to reach the contemplative depth we expect in great literature. But the frequent exceptions capture the undeniable liveliness of the moment: a little girl lifting her dress to reveal her bottom in order to taunt her mother, Spiess haggling over some item at the bustling public market:

> Saturday market:
> a live hen in the scale tray
> -my tomatoes next[54]

or the pathos of a recognizable emotion, for example, leaving a loved spot:

> Last day at the cove
> -a little snowman of sand
> left facing the sea[55]

This last haiku is movingly supported by a charming *haiga* of a sand snowman with a tiny shadow staring out to an enormous expanse of sea, and reflects the appealing light tone found throughout the work.

Although a number of collections of travel haiku, except for the lack of accompanying prose narrative description, resemble the best classical Japanese travel haibun in their subtlety and depth, we perhaps have only one travel haibun that approaches the mood and tone of such classical work. This volume is Tom Lynch's *Rain Drips from the Trees: Haibun along the trans-Canadian Highway* (1992). This collection consists of one long haibun describing a hitchhiking trip from Pennsylvania into Ontario Province and west across Canada to British Columbia and four short haibun on hikes into the mountains and forests of Oregon and Arizona. The title piece, like Bashō's *Narrow Path to the Interior*, includes interesting encounters with people met along the way as well as meditative responses to cityscapes, landscapes, wild

nature, and the process of travelling itself. An entrance into Lynch's haibun occurs in "Autumn at the Valley's Edge," a short haibun on Mt.
Pisgah, Oregon. The second-last paragraph ends: "It is our instinct to
be remote."[56] Lynch is voicing the axiom that allows him to breach the
world of, particularly, nonhuman subjectivities. Nature sets up barriers
to such breaches that we must intuitively respect, notwithstanding the
modern world's reinforcement, even encouragement, of our objectifying
nonhuman nature as mere things to appropriate. Lynch concretizes his
axiom of natural separation and his tacit protectiveness of that separation in the conclusion to this haibun:

> I notice, far down the hill, that the deer have stepped out of the
> trees and stand silently in a clearing.

> far down the slope
> a few deer feed—between us
> rain begins to fall[57]

Despite his conviction of the gulf between individual subjectivities,
Lynch is continually registering the very mystery of how things exist as
such in a given moment and whether such subjectivities exist separate-
ly from his observation of them. He unravels this problem dramatically
in "Climbing Kachina Peaks," a narrative of his trip to these Arizona
mountains that are sacred to the Hopi Native Americans. One of the first
haiku voices the problem:

> car suddenly here,
> suddenly gone—
> dark mountain silence[58]

On descending the mountain he has climbed, toward the end of his trip, he restates the problem in terms of nonhuman nature:

> suddenly here
> grasshopper on my knee
> suddenly gone[59]

Lynch finally resolves the problem in his conclusion to the haibun:

> Thinking of a shower, and hot supper, and how to write this, I hike through forest I don't notice. Now, after shower, and supper, and writing this, I think of forest I missed.

> > cold moonlight
> > on kachina peaks—
> > if I step outside, if I don't[60]

The peaks, like everything else in nature, have their own intrinsic existences, regardless of what human consciousness might hold or not hold on the matter.

Yet in Lynch's haibun, and in nature itself, there seems a protective distance separating human consciousness from the true natures of nonhuman existences. It is as if our own subjectivity fosters such protectiveness in nonhuman subjectivities. In any event, the main theme of his long title haibun appears to be the impossibility of breaching in some final way this protectiveness. However, nature itself seems at times to elicit communion with itself, as in this early haiku:

almost asleep
a breeze wakes me—
northern lights[61]

But this communion throughout the haibun is never complete, perhaps underscoring an indefinite quality of mystery inherent in intra-subjective exchanges with nonhuman nature. In such exchanges our normal orientation toward normal dimensional coordinates and psychologically felt experience is undermined. Thus the strongest sections of the work record descriptive moments of physical distance, like the northern lights of this haiku or the loon diving in the distance in another;[62] transitional moments of going to sleep and waking up, as in this haiku; or eerie moments in which animals are awake while the author sleeps,[63] such as:

dream under stars—
an elk's breath
mists the darkness[64]

They also record atmospheric indefiniteness, as in a haiku on rain-soaked trees in misty twilights[65] or this on a reoriented sea gull:

dense mist—
in dawn light a gull
again finds land[66]

This haibun does not resolve the mystery of such indefiniteness but tries to simply poetically record or celebrate it. At its conclusion, echoing Whitman's breaching of eternity in "Crossing Brooklyn Ferry," Lynch engages in a more traditional way Lifshitz's concern with the limits of human perception and consciousness:

Victoria, buy a few peaches, toss pits into the sea. To what avail time, waiting for the ferry.

> cross the straits
> through evening blue
> venus behind thin clouds

I lean on the rail. Tonight too, crossing Victoria ferry, white sea gulls high in the air float with motionless wings. To what avail space.[67]

But, more importantly, Lynch's haibun as a whole are a testament, beyond the question of the failures of human subjectivity, of the revelatory subjectivities in nature which—though partially hidden, like the star in this haiku—are nonetheless waiting for our aesthetic contact.

A volume as strong as *Rain Drips from the Trees* is Penny Harter's *At the Zendō* (1993), a collection of haiku, haibun, and poetry centered on trips to the Dai Bosatsu Zendō, a traditional Zen Buddhist monastery in the Catskill Mountains of upstate New York, and on the act of attaining Buddhist enlightenment. The main section, "A Weekend at Dai Bosatsu Zendō," is a diary of a visit to the monastery in September 1987, beginning with the picking up of friends at Grand Central Station in New York City and ending with Harter's departure from the monastery. This haibun records Harter's gradual induction into the way of life and, finally, the consciousness of a Zen Buddhist monastery, registering Harter's gradual awakening into a Zennian consciousness through the more and more subtle presentations of her responses to her thoughts and perceptions.

A key passage occurs at the first morning meditation. After an hour of chanting sutras while walking rapidly with the other residents, a period of silent sitting meditation, and ten minutes of collective silent walking, Harter and the others begin silent sitting meditation again:

> Another half hour of zazen. No time passes, and at the gong my eyes start open to see each thing distinct, luminous, itself.
>
> after meditation
> one leaf settles
> into the grass
>
> sunrise—
> tree trunks
> dividing mist
>
> Chanting, we file in, to a silent breakfast. Unfolding the cloth that covers the chopsticks and nested lacquer bowls we carried from the meditation hall, we place chopsticks on our right, tips angled off the table's edge, separate the bowls, all following last night's instructions.
>
> just oatmeal in the bowl—
> oatmeal glistening
> in the bowl[68]

This passage reveals the process whereby Harter's consciousness is transformed so by meditation that she begins to see things, in the Zennian phrase, just as they are, without the intervention of subjective consciousness: a leaf simply falls to the grass, trees simply appear out of the mist, oatmeal simply sits in its bowl.

This newly won awareness carries over through a hectic day and night of activity as memory:

I lie quietly, remembering the presence in the corner of the dining hall:

> evening meditation
> the jade plant sits
> next to its reflection[69]

This entrance into universal subjectivity also registers the Buddhist idea of compassion for all living things when, the next day, Harter visits the monastery cemetery:

> climbing to the stupa—
> not stepping on
> the red salamander[70]

In this encounter while visiting an important monastery teacher's grave, we also sense a hint of the teacher's spirit incarnated in this simple creature, a moment just as it is, but resonating all the more deeply with Buddhist reality.

The haibun concludes with Harter's departure and an expression of her newly found compassion and consciousness:

> among the trees
> somewhere rain falling
> on the doe's back
>
> coming down
> so many more leaves
> have turned[71]

Harter's compassion for other subjectivities is extended to the doe in the rain. Time has passed since Harter entered the zendō. More autumn leaves have taken on bright color. Nothing much else has changed externally. Yet, for Harter, for her consciousness, everything has changed.

This change remains with Harter into the next year. After a haiku retreat at Spring Lake, New Jersey, Harter returns to her home and begins sitting meditation:

> ...at once tears rolling down my cheeks, *knowing* we are only this, only precisely what we are doing at any given moment, no more; we are as transparent as the leaf in sunlight. Nothing matters because nothing exists. Our houses are just paper boxes blown down around us—our bodies are just paper bags blown in around us. Inside we go in and up—we are nothing except everything else. I truly don't know who, better yet *what* I am, what *we* are, all of us peopling, infinite variety, yet all the same, since I (we) don't exist except in the moment, constantly changing.[72]

Alluding perhaps to the statement attributed to Bashō that haiku is what is happening at a given place at a given moment, Harter here offers the highwater mark for English-language haibun as a revelation of spiritual consciousness.

In a lighter vein, but with a serious underlying motif, is *Met on the Road: A Transcontinental Haiku Journey* by William J. Higginson and Penny Harter (1993). The work records the authors' relocation from Scotch Plains, New Jersey to Santa Fe, New Mexico, beginning with a meeting of the Haiku Society of America in New York City and ending with Higginson's trip to a Haiku North America convention in California just after their arrival in Santa Fe. At both the meeting and the convention, and along the way to Santa Fe, the authors collected haiku from people they visited with. The work thus incidentally becomes an anthology of haiku by some of the strongest contemporary American haiku poets.

The light, but bittersweet, tone of the work is established by the presence of the authors' pet cat, which becomes an icon of the home they will probably never return to. The mood of nostalgia is introduced the night before they leave:

> Finally, around midnight, we begin packing the car—in the garage for the first time since we moved into the house. Don't forget Purr, the eight-year-old cat.
>
> > the neighborhood
> > silent under streetlamps—
> > a thin mist[73]

The pain of nostalgia heats up at a stop in Pennsylvania:

> > does he even know us
> > this cat after months
> > in a cage
>
> > purring cat—
> > how long ago in Paterson
> > your littermate died

> Occasionally blurting out, "What could we do?" we drove to our evening's stop.... Getting ready for bed, we close the door and turn Purr loose in our room for the night, setting the pattern that we'll follow for the next several days. From our old house, 320 miles.

the cat stares down

from the second-floor window:

crickets[74]

Until they reach Santa Fe, the marking of the distance from their home occurs intermittently as a refrain of nostalgia. Purr is obviously a soothing icon of the comfort of domesticity even when he is naughty, as when, for the first time on the trip, Purr causes a minor catastrophe by breaking a host's ceramic bowl. Lamenting their letting their guard down, the authors only half-seriously scold themselves: "We should have known: Never take your cat for granted."[75]

The serious motif concerns the relation of haiku to ecology. The motif is introduced while the authors are visiting with the haiku poet Lee Gurga and his family. During a discussion of Patricia Donegan's essay "Haiku & the Ecotastrophe," collected in the anthology *Dharma Gaia*, Higginson has a flash of recognition and quotes from the essay:

When she writes of her study of season words with the elderly Japanese haiku master Seishi Yamaguchi, Pat goes on to express the very ideal that deepened my own commitment to haiku a decade ago when I was writing *The Haiku Handbook*:

Stopping the ecocrisis, eliminating the bomb, or spreading the world's wealth more equitably [are] directly connected to stopping our own greed, aggressive tendencies and overconsumptive habits. The activities and personal habits of human beings…contribute most powerfully to the ecological imbalance and destruction of nature's ecosystems. Even the writing of one haiku, and therefore some recognition of our interconnectedness, is a small positive step beyond self-interest.[76]

The motif enters again on Higginson's trip to Haiku North America where part of his talk at the convention will discuss the relation of haiku to the environment. During a visit with James W. Hackett, author of *The Zen Haiku and other Zen Poems of J. W. Hackett*, Higginson again recognizes his own ideas when Hackett "expresses his concern for the environment, saying that he hopes haiku will help us recognize the equality of all species."[77]

Higginson's major insight into this motif occurs while he is thinking about a *senryu* from *The Gulf Within*, an anthology of haiku and senryu on the Gulf War that was published by the Haiku Poets of Northern California. He meditates on the internal nature of war, which might be conceived of as violent thought and emotion, and quotes from one of Marianne Moore's poems on this theme: "never was a war that was/not inward." Finally, he relates these lines of poetry to his thinking on the connection of haiku to our relation to the nonhuman world and ourselves to produce one of our most profound expressions of haiku poetics.

If we could but bring this kind of insight, each day, to ourselves and our fellow human creatures, perhaps there would be fewer occasions for wars without. The haiku to face, unblinking, the natural world we must each make peace with and live within; the senryu to face, unblinking, the inner lives we must each somehow make more human, more natural.[78]

In a way the prose descriptions and haiku conceived and collected on Higginson's and Harter's transcontinental journey are testaments to the kind of internal adjustment Higginson is calling for. Just before the authors reach Santa Fe, they encounter their first accident. They are more careful of their driving from then on but the haiku, or rather senryu, precipitated by the accident becomes a final wry comment, even objective correlative, of the difficulties in but nonetheless utmost importance of adjusting our relation to the natural world and to our own postmodern culture in its implicit comment on the presumptions mankind and its technology take in regard to wild nature:

> under the sign
> warning of falling rocks
> a car struck the mountain[79]

A final chapbook-length haibun, of note for its relation to traditional Japanese journals, is Brent Partridge's unpublished *Road through the Stars*, an account of his encounters with nonhuman nature in California preceding the beginning of a teaching assignment in Japan. The second entry, dated February 24, 1994, reflects the delicate tone of Partridge's relation to nature as he offers his rationale for his journal:

Waking in the middle of the night in my old room at my folk's place, now called the bead-room. I've thought of a title for a travel diary. Here where the towns join one another the sky is light enough to write without turning on a light or opening the curtains and so I do.

> On a chilly night
> Preparing for an endless journey
> A star through the curtains.

This room where I've awakened again and again in dreams when somewhere else.

Without the inspiration of a Japanese poet of long ago I probably wouldn't be beginning this diary, something I've always previously shrunk from...which leads me to think of the combustion patterns of stars and in turn of the different ways that time may be said to have effect.

The dark, sweet fragrance of the elms is comforting, restful.[80]

Alluding perhaps specifically to Bashō's *Narrow Path to the Interior* and to his example as a travelling poet, Partridge prepares himself internally for his journey to Japan. His more direct influence, however, is Thoreau. In an early entry Partridge almost paraphrases Thoreau's explanation for his experiment at Walden Pond: "My strategy of life—to live simply, enjoy myself close to nature."[81] The journal's final entry before Partridge leaves for Japan is in fact a quotation from Thoreau's *A Week on the Concord and Merrimack Rivers.*[82]

Like Thoreau and Bashō, Partridge wishes to maintain an intimate contact with nonhuman nature. Accordingly, most of the journal takes place in secluded dwellings deep in nature or in wild nature itself. An early entry in such a dwelling establishes the ambiguous relation between Partridge and nature:

Wild creatures scraping
The corner of a window
—Lonely winter night.

Loneliness is not a matter of solitude, but of juxtaposition. An old house far from the neighbors or a phone, with the rain and wind being some of the friendlier visitors, and none are invited in.[83]

At first Partridge's human subjectivity keeps him at a distance from nonhuman nature, as he strives for a deeper Bashō-like objective contact. This subjectivity anthropomorphizes nature in its juxtaposition to Partridge and human culture: an elk herd seems to think that Partridge's hat has horns,[84] a mouse eats a bar of soap because it is supposedly dumb,[85] mating fish and some motionless deer are contrasted with the end of the holiday season.[86] Later, a transitional haiku establishes a division between human subjectivity and the "objectivity" of nature:

> Deep in the country
> The daffodils have more glow
> Than they do in town[87]

But on a rock-hunting hike shortly before leaving for Japan Partridge manages to bridge the gap to that "objectivity":

> Agates, wildflowers—
> Just under a mountaintop
> Crowned with laurel[88]

This "objectivity" leads to a sense of compassion for natural subjectivity that, on a final hike in California, can allow for a reconciliation of sorts with the unthinking human appropriation of nonhuman nature:

> forgive the firebreak
> considering how well
> the wildflowers like it[89]

Partridge is, as his sensitive published nature haiku attest, on the side of nonhuman subjectivities. This consciousness carries over to his landing in Japan:

> As the plane touched down, the runway lined with the prettiest flowering cherries I've ever seen—at their peak.
> Flowering cherries scattered along the highway continuously halfway to this airport. Japan's far more beautiful at this first glimpse than I'd imagined. Invigorating.
>
> Foot-high whitecaps on the Sumida River.
>
> A friendly Airport Limousine-Bus porter laughing refuses my tip.
>
> > With a schedule change
> > Missing visiting a friend
> > —Still—cherries blossom[90]

And by his first day in Japan, Partridge has adopted a relation to non-human nature that reflects a decidedly Buddhist respect for such realities which, in the Western world, would be considered animistic:

> > bowing to a crow
> > it lifts its beak a little—
> > the trees are still bare[91]

The transference of Partridge's newly won consciousness of universal subjectivities from California to Japan, though seemingly extraordinary in the context of being in an exotic place where even the crows go, according to Partridge, "'ah-ah' or 'ha-ha,'" rather than "caw-caw,"[92] could be understood analogously with respect to the concept in religious mysticism of achieving a moment of enlightenment that changes a given individual for life. But most people, including poets, cannot but be affected by strange and exotic locales in a manner that would alter their objectivity, or, as poets, their imaginative focus. One, despite the Romantic poet's concern with "negative capability," would naturally see more easily into the essence of an experience that is a familiar part of daily existence. As Robert Spiess notes in his discussion of haiku travel sequences, "…haiku poets write their best haiku, generally speaking, in an environment which is imbued in them—an environment they feel in their bones or solar plexus—not one in which they are attracted by novelty."[93] Many published English-language haibun, accordingly, express a deeply felt identification with a familiar place or person.

Frank Trotman's "Early Morning," a light-toned description of a sunrise at the end of the summer in his home town, is an example. His familiarity with dawn in this particular place allows him to register a sensitive homespun impression of the shifts from summer to fall and from night to day through images of light, sound, stillness, and activity that naturally reflect such a moment in such a place, like the sound of his neighbor's screen door slamming and, shortly after, the presence of the neighbor's tiny white spaniel that "scampers about, here and there, trying out space, barking at silence."[94] Yet the sense of indefiniteness evoked by this deeply felt ordinary moment provokes in Trotman an uncanny mood figuratively expressed as a surreal personification of the powerful natural correlatives underlying such emotion:

In our town the suburban streets are quiet and deserted at this hour. It's as though they stretched on and on to some dim infinity. From time to time a night bird will worry the stillness with tired little notes.

> Unheard—
> roots tightening
> their grips around stones.[95]

Here nature, almost in anguish, prepares itself for a most extraordinary and yet quite commonplace thing so recognizably presented in this haibun: dawn and the rousing of life in an American town.

Two haibun link their response to a familiar place, one most urban, the other rural, to a recollected memory from childhood. Cor van den Heuvel's "Curbstones" is a rumination on the curbstones of New York City and the memory of stones observed in their natural settings during his childhood spent in Maine and New Hampshire. The curbstones thus become for van den Heuvel a subjective urban metaphor of wild nature:

> Each spring I fall in love with granite curbstones. These natural-looking rough-cut stones with their slightly rippled surfaces, their precise and monolithic solidities lining and defining a street from here to infinity, have for me the mysterious presence of mountains, the strange, halted stillness of great glacial deposits: at once stopped and journeying—waiting millennia, yet instantaneously moving through space with their star, our star.[96]

These urban artifacts betray their identities as objects quarried from natural landscapes. In their new settings they, here as curbstones, evoke feelings associated with nature haiku when they reveal their true natures. As van den Heuvel notes: "There is a stillness about them on chilly, rainy days in spring or autumn that suggests such origins."[97] His rumination ends with a description of the emotions in his childhood he associates with curbstones, which become a symbol of natural process that van den Heuvel carries into his adulthood. He thus concludes: "I am still drawn to granite curbstones, and in all seasons of the year...."[98]

Christopher Herold also fuses his meditation, "Scarecrows," with childhood emotion. The context of this haibun is Herold's teaching elementary school children how to build scarecrows. He appends a group of haiku on scarecrows to his description of his work with the children. Most of these convey the humor often evoked by individual scarecrows:

> no birds on the wires:
> a Richard Nixon mask
> > on the scarecrow

> neighbor boy
> > peeping up
> > > the scarecrow's dress[99]

His work with the children calls up the memory of his childhood's self shooting holes with a BB gun into his father's jacket, which covered their family's scarecrow. The recollected young Herold suddenly feels that he has somehow abused his father, so the next day he trades the gun in for a baseball glove. But his childhood's rurally colored sense of a universally animated world remains as his final thought:

after shooting him

apologizing

to the scarecrow[100]

Decidedly urban in tone is Patrick Frank's "Return to Springfield: Urban Haibun," a short narrative of Frank's visit to an outdoor ghetto basketball court where he used to play. Frank sardonically criticizes this Massachusetts city's so-called urban renewal success through the squalor of the court that he depicts in haiku such as this:

the shattered pieces

of a transistor

radio[101]

Frank, the unemployed self-proclaimed Southern Caucasian, plays a pick-up game of basketball with an unemployed black man who, like Frank, would like to return to Springfield but cannot find work. The decay of urban society represented by the court and the two men's social condition is ameliorated by the friendship generated by their chance encounter.

Liz Fenn's "Big Bucks on Tug Hill" also offers us a glimpse of a subculture—small-town, rural New York State. What is described, often in the colloquial rural language they speak, is a card game among some friends who have just finished hunting deer. They are discussing the war years and the draft, which, in their words, "just plain old swept them all away almost overnight...."[102] The focus of the haibun is a narrative within the narrative concerning one hunter's successful ruse to be exempted from the draft. The synchronicity of the end of this fellow's story with his revealing his winning hand establishes a humorous, folksy tone that is also evoked in the concluding haiku in which the man posts his girlfriend's house during hunting season.[103]

Family members or close friends have been used as successful subjects for haibun. Two examples of such haibun concern dying relatives. Cathy Drinkwater Better's "Father-in-Law" narrates a visit to her relative who is undergoing chemotherapy for cancer. The prose description and haiku emphasize the decimated nature of the father-in-law's body and the pathos of the juxtaposition of his condition with his concern for his grandchildren. The hospital overlooks a harbor and one of Better's haiku captures the emotionally charged nature of the father-in-law's mental and physical frailty by contrasting it with the boats in the harbor:

> contemplating his legacy
> in silence, one speedboat
> crosses another's[104]

The ambiguity of what is being crossed—another speedboat's wake or the silence of that distant speedboat created by the quiet, air-conditioned hospital room—provides a strong correlative of the old man's moving toward death.

After a description of his grandfather's early history in Ireland and later history as a United States postman, Rich Youmans in "Sunday Visits" covers the same subject matter as Better. The vitality of his grandfather's early life is contrasted with young Youmans's visits to his grandfather after he has suffered a crippling second stroke. The pathos of the grandfather's condition of mental and physical collapse, in which he

simply stares into the fireplace, is underscored by the contrastive echoing of an earlier description of his childhood nights spent listening to his
own grandfather's stories in "the sweet smell of peat fires"[105] of his present occupation before the fireplace, which in turn is further highlighted
by the concluding haiku.

> twilight…
>
> shadows seep into
>
> grandfather's quiet[106]

Another form of haibun that is at times identified as such by *Modern
Haiku* offers subjective responses to someone else's haiku in a mode that
resembles what once was called impressionistic criticism. The two most
recognizable writers in this category are Tom Tico and Patricia
Neubauer, both of whom respond to Japanese as well as contemporary
American haiku. What they are doing is more in line with traditional
Japanese criticism of haiku, which is highly subjective, than with the
objective critical approaches of the West.

In "Bird Song and Bare Branches" Tom Tico presents what he
calls a "reading" of twelve haiku by Jane Reichhold.[107] Of the twelve
"readings" only one, on thin winter tea, comes even close to what might
be termed an objective response to the images—one that many readers
would naturally come to when responding to its images because a given
interpretation is obviously elicited by those images. The other eleven
"readings" are imaginative conjectures about the intentions of the author
and the possible references for the indefinite images. Number twelve will
serve as an example:

winter twilight

gathers in her lap

white folded hands

As the old woman gazes upon the austere beauty of the winter twilight, she feels an acceptance of her approaching death which manifests in her folded hands that rest upon her lap. And as the twilight advances...her white folded hands become more and more noticeable against her black dress, creating a striking aesthetic effect, but more importantly, emphasizing the resignation and peacefulness that pervade her being.[108]

There is no absolute reason to assume that the woman in the haiku is old, nor to offer the detail of her black dress or her presumed emotional state. But the prose narrative in itself offers an emotionally justified, compelling poetic description of an old woman, however far from the author's original intention for the haiku.

Tico offers a similar "reading" of Shiki's haiku in "In the Spirit of the Samurai" that relies heavily on interpreting the haiku in the context of Shiki's illness and supposed adherence to samurai values. Again, of the twelve haiku considered, only three, numbers four, five, and seven, have interpretations that are clearly objectively related to the haiku. The others offer interpretations that purportedly enter Shiki's mind at the moment of the conception of the given haiku. Tico is not merely addressing Shiki's intention, but his very thoughts and deliberations, which again make for compelling, if at times melodramatic, narrative. The tenor of such narrative may be exemplified in this:

> The scarecrow
>
> Plants his feet in the flood,
>
> Enduring it all.

With the rain pouring down and his feet in the water of the rice field, the scarecrow appears to be the exemplar of patience and fortitude. As Shiki gazes upon the stoical figure, he wishes that he too could manifest such poise and equanimity in the face of his own pain and discomfort. He remembers his grandfather, the old samurai, who told him that fearlessness and fortitude were the most important traits that a man could have in meeting the trials of life.[109]

Tico's interpretation touches on the mood of endurance, however ironic, that is carried in the image of the scarecrow. The presentation of Shiki's thought process, particularly his recollection of his grandfather's philosophy, however interesting, is an imaginative leap of biographical clairvoyance unfamiliar to our canon of Western criticism.

Much more accessible to Western sensibilities, and strongly moving, is Tico's "Reaching for the Rain," a meditation on a child's openness to experience. Using other poets' haiku, Tico moves in seven sections from a child's birth and first engagement with the mystery of experience to the probably inevitable loss of childhood's innocence. Each section begins and ends with a haiku. The short prose meditation between them includes a reference to an image from each of the haiku. When they are successful, these prose responses enter the mind of the child in a way that enhances our response to the haiku, all of which are quite strong in their own right, and sets up a cumulative response from us similar to that elicited by Blake's *Songs of Innocence* and *Songs of Experience*. The regimentation of elementary school and the hints at childhood's emotional pain belong to the latter kinds of experience. Innocence is offered in a section on kites:

> Wind
>> tugging a kite
>>> tugging a boy...

>>>> *Bonnie May Malody*

Perhaps the great charm of kite flying is that you feel the kite as an extension of your being; you feel as if your spirit were soaring into the sky. An exhilarating experience—and one which can be enjoyed alone or in the company of others.

> the wind—
>> full of laughter
>>> and kite strings

>>>> *Ross Figgins*[110]

Patricia Neubauer covers the same subject in "The Goldfish Vendor," a response to a haiku by Shuran Takahashi that depicts children following a goldfish vendor down a narrow lane. Neubauer begins her impressionistic response: "The moment of pure delight is an ephemeral thing."[111] She then contrasts the world of the child (and poet) to that of the adult who is unable to share in that delight. Children, unlike adults, are, for Neubauer, "indifferent to the past, unconcerned about the future,"[112] and can thus live in the ecstasy of the living present

moment, like the one offered by the goldfish vendor. In "Primavera"—
a response to a haiku by Matthew Louvière in which a young bag-lady
in a bright poncho wakes up on a rainy spring morning—Neubauer
admits that no one can know exactly how a poet arrived at his or her
haiku, and acknowledges that other readers will come up with different
interpretations of this haiku than hers. For Neubauer, the bag-lady
alludes to the sense of awakening and rebirth that is evoked in
Botticelli's *Primavera* and *The Birth of Venus*. Although we may have difficulty seeing in this haiku the "goddess of spring" that Neubauer sees,
except, perhaps, through bold irony, we all feel the spring-like values of
the youthful bag-lady that she points out to us: "gentleness and fresh-
ness, tenderness and expectancy."[113] In both pieces, the little imaginative prose dramas on the children and the vendor and on the contemporary, though unusual, Venus enrich our emotional response to each
of their respective haiku.

A common, perhaps predominant, theme in American haibun
is one that addresses the nature of childhood, or rather, the memory of
one's own childhood. This should not be surprising when one considers that haibun incorporates the aesthetic values of haiku in its composition. In a passage from Jack Kerouac's *The Dharma Bums* the narrator
observes that he "could understand the perfect gems of haikus the
Oriental poets had written, never getting drunk in the mountains or
anything but just going along fresh as children writing down what they
saw without literary devices or fanciness of expression."[114] One of the
values of haiku, as described here by Kerouac, is a subjective openness
to experience that may be most easily comprehended analogously in
the emotional spontaneity of children. Particularly in postmodern
America such spontaneity might not be easily won by the adult, the

subject of Neubauer's "The Goldfish Vendor." As Kerouac's narrator suggests, one must have an oriental consciousness in order to receive experience like a child. One thinks of the child-like state recommended in Taoism with its emphasis on *wu wei*, an existential passivity, an absence of what we would call the adult will, before experience of the joyous state maintained by Zen Buddhists in their enlightened state of "no mind," an "objective," that is, non-willing, receptivity to the essences of things in their own right. In such states the beauty of experience is evident in itself, just as it is. The expression of such experience as art does not need figurative expression to heighten its impact. The essences, the subjectivities in their own right, will resonate with their own energy, liveliness, joy, moodiness, and the like, as they do in haiku. American haibun attempts to explore how such states are achieved as well as to evoke these states themselves.

In *A Boy's Seasons*, an ongoing haibun serialized in *Modern Haiku* beginning with the Fall 1993 issue, Cor van den Heuvel offers us another but more detailed glimpse into his Norman Rockwell-like childhood on the northern New England coast in the thirties and forties. This haibun is interesting because, in addition to the precisely reconstructed moments of a recognizably typical American boyhood, we are given an account of the development of the sensibility that would, in later life, attach itself to the aesthetics of haiku in the adult haiku theorist. The young van den Heuvel made a Zen-like discipline out of his preoccupation with sports which for him demarcated the comings and goings of the natural seasons. As he notes in the introduction to the work: "This devotion was a kind of religion. With my mind and body totally involved in the practice or playing of these sports I felt a oneness with my surroundings and by extension with the universe...."[115]

The adult haiku poet then reads back onto his childhood experience his mature understanding of oriental sensibility:

first warm day
fitting my fingers into the mitt
pounding the pocket

When it was warm and sunny enough for us to get out a ball and gloves, we knew spring had arrived. A baseball was our plum blossom. We loved the game the way a Japanese haiku poet loves the plum tree, which is the first to bloom in spring. A baseball would come out with gloves or mitts for a game of catch when the ground was still muddy and there was snow lingering under the hedge. It blossomed in the blue skies of early spring, and it would continue to bloom all summer long.

summer afternoon
the long fly ball to center field
takes its time[116]

Like the ball in the concluding haiku, the young van den Heuvel has many moments when, in his words, "everything clicks into place and time seems to stop to take note of it...."[117] Such moments, usually associated with sports or childhood visits to the beach or the circus, were van den Heuvel's only childhood connection to the emotional experience evoked in haiku. In fact, he admits that he didn't experience a "spirit of nature" until he attended college and read the Romantics and the American Transcendentalists, camped in nature, and, later, read Japanese haiku.[118]

But the moments he does record, like Wordsworth's "spots of time," offer us the silliness of childhood:

> long afternoon
> the right fielder is playing
> with a dog[119]

Or the mystery waiting at the edge of immediate experience:

> under the lights
> hitting it out of the park
> and into the night[120]

Or the romantic adventures in hideouts, in playing cowboys and Indians, or, as in the following, at the circus when the child's imaginative horizon is boundless:

> Carrying water to the elephants, camels and other animals made me feel I'd been brought into contact with distant places around the world—places in Africa and Asia. The smells and sounds as well as the look of these animals brought a new sense of the earth into my life: its variety and novelty seemed endless.

> > straw
> > on the elephant's back
> > summer breeze[121]

Or in the willfully mischievous behavior of the young van den Heuvel who audaciously sneaks onto a merry-go-round with his dog.[122]

Another author who explores the nature of childhood and his own childhood's self in as sensitive a manner as van den Heuvel is Tom Clausen. Clausen's unpublished *Going to Grandma's* is an account of a childhood trip from his home in Ithaca, New York to his grandmother's home in Vermont. The humorous narrative center of the account is the fact that Clausen and his sister squabble so persistently during the trip that their mother makes the young Clausen get out of the car and run along the highway until he is too tired to bother his sister. He concludes the piece with an assessment of what such experience really means: "It would take dozens of years for me to realize that it's moments like these that help keep a family together. What I felt that day, long ago, was in a brilliant little bundle of moments what being young is all about."[123] The ostensive conclusion to be drawn is that a child needs to be disciplined for his or her own good. But the narrative itself reveals that this childhood "moment" is really about the anxiety of separation and the testing of a young will.

This psychological complex is introduced when the running young Clausen passes a forest. At first Clausen experiences mild concern but then he creates a romance about the experience—a typical make-believe game of childhood that allows a child to explore his or her emotional nature: "The forest on either side of the road invited glances and the powerful thought that I could just veer off and disappear into those deep woods forever. Wouldn't she be sorry, I smugly imagined...."[124] This complex is repeated when the young Clausen has jogged out of sight of his mother's car. A man in a pickup truck slows down and asks the young boy if he needs a ride. Clausen narrates his response:

> I hesitated, amazed, tempted, but then said, "No, I guess not, I'll be getting a ride with someone soon." I said this half looking back and half wishing I could see the Plymouth, but it wasn't in sight. A slight shiver passed through me. I could have gotten in

the truck; I could have run away, with help. This could have been a pivotal moment heading me into a completely different life.

> a long way
> from home   my pillow
> in the car[125]

Anxiety and romantic imagination working overtime, the young Clausen makes perhaps his first real contact with the existential dilemma of his own existence as such. From such experiences the maturing child will develop a deeper sense of what life really means. But that meaning for the young Clausen is all but supplied by the nurturing family he dreams of escaping. His true feelings, however, are concretized in the longed-for pillow recollected by the adult Clausen in the haiku.

Clausen is also able to examine the emotional terrain of childhood by comparing his own childhood's experience with that of his young son's. Clausen's "New Sneakers" is a light-hearted look at the ritual of buying new sneakers. He amusingly compares his childhood's "plain canvas Skippys bought at five-and-dime stores" to the "large, clumpy, light-up-glaring barges" modern children want.[126] The haibun describes his son's delight with his new footgear, including their first stains. Clausen concludes his haibun with a nod to the emotional depth of a child's joy, one the young Clausen once felt as a child himself:

> …I'll never forget that night when still brand-new these sneakers were the magic of a young heart and mind.

> five-year-old snuggles
> his new sneakers
> in bed[127]

Yet the claims of adult parenthood can undermine one's ability to recapture the felt joy of childhood through a kind of emotional osmosis with one's own child. Clausen's "Before School" narrates the bittersweet struggle of the adult ego with the reality of no longer being a child, what Clausen calls the "old test of self."[128] This phrase intrudes itself in a narrated spat with his wife over who will take their son, who would soon enter kindergarten, to a parent and child get-together. Because of the spat Clausen broods over his adulthood and thus loses emotional contact with his own childhood, ironically spent in the same kindergarten his son will attend:

> The playground...the school, the same one I went to over thirty years earlier, yet somehow heading there had no hold on my imagination or fancy. Instead a slight sullenness and dread filled me at having to make an appearance for some other adults who I feared would be less able than me to honestly confront how hard it is to be...a parent.[129]

It turns out that the Clausens had gotten the date of the gathering wrong, so Tom and his son are free to chase each other around the vacant playground. Clausen concludes the haibun in a haunting confrontation with his loss of childhood whose correlative is a peopleless playground and a solitary butterfly:

> We enjoy the space, the peace and quiet, the setting down day...must be she got the time or week or day...something...
>
> > before school
> > about the empty playground
> > a monarch[130]

American haibun, however far from its origins in Japanese literature, appears to be in the process of discovering its own aims and needs. An engagement with the emotional terrain of the child, so close to the spiritual values of the East, is a necessary facet of this discovery because it allows for a reconstruction of how we, as Western adults, relate to felt experience. The static that one feels under the claims of adulthood, so well addressed by Neubauer and Clausen, offers an impediment to this reconstruction. Yet emotional complexity initiated in childhood is a necessary element in the adult's aesthetic engagement with life. Therefore such emotional complexity is sought for or recollected. If it is not engaged, a kind of emotional unease or even despair undermines our life, as in Clausen's "Before School."

My work "Aglow" addresses the tidal currents of mediating between an undefined adult despair, provoked by days of sunless November weather, and the recollection of childhood wonderment, associated in the haibun with Keats's "magic casements," my own childhood viewing of the animated film *Alice in Wonderland*, and the contemporary film *The Secret Garden*, a version of the classic children's story.[131] The despair is evoked through images of early winter rain and decay:

November rain—
the outdoor jack-o'-lantern
collapsing on itself[132]

I attempt to raise my own spirits by seeing *The Secret Garden*. The film rekindles memories of my father taking me as a small child to see *Alice in Wonderland*:

We had walked in after the film had begun. It was one of my first trips to the movies. What I remember is entering a sacred special place. The dark theater demanding a sense of awe. And there at the end of the tunnel of darkness the magical animated figures in brilliant pastel colors—a figuration from another dimension. Of dream. Of spirit.[133]

After attending to mundane adult activities, I bridge the gap between adult despair and childhood enchantment through what could be called a haiku moment or, in other terms, an epiphany, an occasion of deep spiritual revelation:

> On the way home on the expressway my attention suddenly was drawn to a haze of flame at the horizon. The late afternoon light was collected in the top of the stand of naked trees on the horizon. I was somehow transported to some other dimension. I remembered the smile I had when I left *The Secret Garden* last night. I was, in some intangible way, home:
>
> > late afternoon light—
> > the stand of bare trees aglow
> > on the horizon[134]

Thus, in some mysterious way memories of my childhood consciousness provoke a transformation of my adult emotional state of undefined moodiness. This in turn provides a general emotional openness before experience that connects me to a revelation of natural subjectivity that is unmediated by the worldly-wise adult mind. It also dispels my sense of dejection through this aesthetic revelation that is so close to that of the Taoist-like receptivity of a child to the subjectivities of nonhuman nature.

Yet a transformation through a connection with the child's consciousness, so often evoked in American haibun, or through a Zen-like awakening such as that described by Harter, is not a common component of our aesthetic experience. We need to arrive at our adult epiphanies, moreover, without predicating them too often upon our direct connection with childhood or a foregrounded spiritual practice, making these elements the dominant subject of our revelation. We need to meet our adult experience through a mature aesthetic consciousness that is determined anew by the particularity of each given experience in and of itself. And if we move toward a higher mature awareness of nonhuman nature in the meeting of our epiphanies, we will also be moving toward a higher mature awareness of human nature in the most profound sense.

Rich Youmans's "For My Wife on Our First Anniversary" exemplifies deep-felt adult experience as revelation. In early spring Youmans wakes at dawn to observe his sleeping wife. His recorded perceptions and thoughts make this haibun, which is deeply Christian in its allusions, an aubade, or morning love lyric. What Youmans experiences is an epiphany of the essential meaning of his life with his new wife as both eros, or physical passion, and agape, or spiritual passion. As he declares early in the haibun: "This is our life together...."[135] What causes this thought is the beauty he sees in his sleeping wife. She murmurs in her sleep, beginning to awaken, like the dawn and the new season of rebirth. This awakening is underscored by an allusion to the Resurrection in the dogwood petals outside the window, which are described as "cruciform."[136] Youmans' epiphany is evoked through a figurative spiritualization of the material world by the morning light which, in a potent metaphor, is transformed by the window glass into rainbows touching various things in the bedroom, as if to show the husband how to comprehend reality and the life he is living with his wife. He is being shown that his true life is much richer than even the beauty experienced in his physical love for his wife:

> Slowly, the sky brightens; sunlight washes our room, breaks through window prisms into tiny rainbows. I search them out as if on an Easter egg hunt: one on the frame of the standing mirror; another on my chest of drawers, under the photos of us laughing and hugging. And others—on my nightstand, the cedar chest, the Japanese lantern hanging over our bed....[137]

His wife begins to wake up. As if being taught a final lesson about true love he watches a rainbow appear on his wife's cheek as she wakes up. He fuses eros and agape by kissing that cheek. And the haibun ends with their making love:

> prisms in
> early light:
> we make love[138]

William M. Ramsey explores in "Gurdjieff, Zen, and Meher Baba" the other side of our deep attachments to each other in this record of the aftermath of the death of his young child. This masterful work is divided into four sections. The first records the burial, a Lycidas-like undermining of nature, and the author's rejection of traditional Christian ritual. The author's despair is poignantly evoked through figurative expression throughout the work. Here at the beginning of the haibun he describes burying the coffin in emotionally wrenching metaphors: "...my infant's little box, lighter than a shovelful of soggy dirt this early December dusk, yet heavier than a pile of laundered diapers."[139] Ramsey introduces the theme of the undermining of the natural world's peace, a correlative of his emotional collapse, through three powerful similes: a vine choking a pine tree, a worm "impaled" by a fishing hook, and a deer caught in a leghold trap.[140] The young corpse, likewise, through metaphor, becomes a "felled tree" or "a dead rat in a culvert's mouth."[141] Finally, he tacitly rejects Catholicism as a means of solace in a moving simile on his child's dead body: "…irrelevant to his brown irises glinting, in blank hospital silence, like rosary beads left scattered in a salt desert."[142]

The short second section repeats the theme of the undermining of nature. Ramsey gets up from a nap with his wife in order to find some deeper consolation in a walk along the beach. What he encounters is an emblem of his vision of nature as predation in another metaphor of his despair:

> the gull dives in,
> lifting to heaven
> an angry fish[143]

In the third section the author at last finds some comfort by working in his garden. This turn of emotion is highlighted by his observing a dung beetle eating straw embedded in some animal's excrement. He marvels at the economy of the natural world in which nothing is wasted and plans to tell his wife about his realization. But minutes later he is undermined again when he accidentally spears a toad while turning compost.

The fourth and final section records Ramsey's spiritual metamorphosis, however tentative, through the metaphoric regeneration of physical desire for food and sexual love. These metaphors moreover mark a literal Buddhist-like transformation of the author's relation to the world. To transform his dark vision of nature he must, like a Buddhist, extend compassion to all living things. Thus he has moved toward a vegetarian diet. He will not be responsible for the death of other beings. This turn is marked by a haiku on his reverence for all life:

> a stiff raccoon
> praying for his error
> by the roadside[144]

Ramsey's epiphany is the awareness that what he observed in nature, in the example of the beetle, is true: all things are interrelated and we must show compassion to all those things. We must not kill them. We must not eat them. But death nonetheless occurs.

When he sees some hams displayed in a farmers' market he becomes depressed again. But the last part of the haibun records his very Western and very human compromise with the fact of death. Many of us cannot simply accept the death of those we care for, including, in an expanded circle of love and compassion, nonhuman creatures. Most of us cannot see the force of reincarnation or the simple fate of matter in the death of that which we love. So there is enormous integrity in Ramsey's deeply moving artistic honesty in relation to spiritual thought and practice:

> But in this dusk, in this nightly rite of urgent flesh and yet more hungry spirit, our hearts find solace in broccoli, carrots, onions— and in one level cup of rice, poured in precise and needed measure. Then, over tea, we talk of Gurdjieff, Zen, and Meher Baba—pretending to assume, once again, that life is sweet as well as rare. Later, at midnight,

her hair smell
in my face, my fingers
count her vertebrae[145]

Ramsey has come to cherish the simple things most close to him—a shared meal, a shared bed. And though these things cannot dispel death and the loss of what he loves, they can dispel the melancholy which, if given a chance, would undermine all of experience and all of the simple things he loves. And with each act of compassion, with each little prayer, with each gesture toward love, with each deeply felt haiku, the self-perpetuating claims of that old despair will be in some final way undermined. Through its evocation of such actions, "Gurdjieff, Zen, and Meher Baba" becomes exemplary of what American haibun should be moving toward.

English literature does not provide suitable prose and poetry models for exploring heightened states of emotion, such as those embodied in the Japanese literary tradition that includes *The Tale of Genji*, *Narrow Path to the Interior*, and the fiction of Soseki, although Wordsworth's *The Prelude* and "Tinturn Abbey," much of Whitman's poetry, and the fiction of Kerouac establish benchmarks in lyric poetry's need to engage itself with prose narrative. Accordingly, the emerging concerns of contemporary American haibun, expressed in more serious as well as lighter tonalities, appear to be four-fold: to poetically chronicle events as they happen, to respond impressionistically to other writers' poetic expressions, to explore poetic experience lodged in one's memory, and to express moments of deep personal revelation. These concerns, moreover, as with the English Romantic poets, often center on the natural world and childhood.

We might contrast the aims, in their highest valences, of haibun and haiku to help elucidate further the aesthetic nature of haibun.

Essentially, haibun is a detailed narrative of experience while haiku is only a moment of pinpointed emotion. During a discussion generated by a haiku workshop at the 1994 Haiku Society of America Retreat at Dai Bosatsu Zendō, Marshall Hryciuk, president of Haiku Canada, noted that one of the failures of modern English haiku is that it attempts to create a little drama. Haiku, thus, because it is a nonnarrative poetic form, invites an extraordinary act of reception from the reader of haiku. A haiku is a moment of unexplained emotion. To respond to it the reader must reexperience the emotional complex of the author. In effect, the reader must complete the haiku by emotionally responding to the ambiguity and mystery of the one or two simple images which apparently had a profound effect on the author. Since the effect is not explained or exhaustively obvious, the reader must enter the emotional complex of the images to recover the emotion generated in the author at the creation of the given haiku. In haibun the narrative direction of the prose is almost always specific enough to make its aesthetic intent, and that of any accompanying haiku, clearly evident. At its best, haibun offers us a narrative of the process of arriving at a given revelation which is highlighted by the figurative and sound values of its prose and the depth of its haiku. In this understanding of the form a haibun is a narrative of an epiphany. Haiku, on the other hand, offers us an epiphany, a revelation. It is a mere node of emotionally charged images that record emotion felt in a given moment in a given place without explanation, without narrative, without figurative adornment. It offers revelation in and of itself.

Yet there is a need for the kind of aesthetic experience haibun provides. There is a vacuum in English literature because there is no strong tradition of truly poetic prose. Haibun provides us with a form that allows us to explore our most deeply felt experience at length and as a process. As such it offers us a diary of epiphanies.

Baudelaire created prose poetry—and perhaps in the process, as many critics would have it, modern poetry—through his rejection of a classicism of poetic form and content that wouldn't allow him to explore, to a deep subconscious level, his own emotional experience. In a like manner haibun offers the contemporary English language poet a way of expressing his intimate lyric consciousness in a more profound way than that provided by the tepid poetic narratives evoked in much contemporary American poetry. But whereas Baudelaire appealed to surrealist and expressionist figurations in his attempt to evoke his passionately searched for, often subliminal, internal emotional experience, contemporary American haibun writers, as heirs to the Japanese tradition of this form, appeal to a "higher," more Zennian emotional consciousness which, for the most part, tries to reckon with a deeply felt engagement with experience as such, however they might heighten it with poetic expression and narrative interest, to arrive at and express their epiphanies.

In a discussion of the Taoist inclination to withdraw from "artificial civilization to pursue one's own inner nature" in order to explore a state of "non-action" or *wu-wei* in one's "communion with nature,"[146] Professor Chong Sun Kim of the University of Rhode Island notes:

Contemporary man has come to the sad state where he is separate from nature, his fellow man, and from his own self. Selfishness and narrowness are the root causes of many a modern problem of our society and state. Instead of improving our within, we frantically attempt to improve our without and the result is disastrous.[147]

Professor Chong Sun Kim is describing here the schizophrenic condition of what has been termed the postmodern condition. With respect specifically to the United States this condition was inevitable.

In the perhaps short history of this perhaps most influential nation's pursuance of its inner spiritual history, it came to a juncture. The United States from its inception was heir to its Puritan heritage of austerity in emotion and industry in action. An engagement with the activities of labor and the development of a newly settled continent predominated. Nature was relegated to a dramatic allegory of good and evil. And fueled by the mercantile spirit of the eighteenth century with its ultimate reliance upon the efficacy of reason, the nexus of the American identity became what it remains today—an unlimited commitment to the production and appropriation of materiality. In the demotic, America had adopted its "go-get-'em" spirit. However, in the early nineteenth century, a contrary understanding of the American spirit realized itself. Perhaps first engaged at the beginning of that century by the then-renowned poet William Cullen Bryant (1794–1878), this new direction was American Transcendentalism. Bryant's *Thanatopsis* (1817) had been received as the first great literary poem in America. This and his other poems, relying on Bryant's reading of the English Romantics with their evocation of sublime moments felt in profound exchanges with the natural world, led to a dominant transformation at least in the world of literature, of how we perceived nature. Ralph Waldo Emerson (1803–1882) was the philosopher of this new spirit. In poems like "The Rhodora" and "Each and All" and in essays like *Nature* and *The Over-Soul*, Emerson expressed his idea that there is a "fundamental unity" between man and nature. In a dialectic with nature, according to Emerson, we make contact with the Over-Soul, an ultimate spiritual force that unites all things. Nature is thus somehow a reflection of human spirituality. Emerson and American Transcendentalism legitimized the idea that our claims for exploring our true inner spirit were more important than the claims of an endless pursuit of the material.

Henry David Thoreau was Emerson's secretary. On Independence Day, July 4, 1845, Thoreau spent his first night in his cabin at Walden Pond. *Walden* records his two-year exploration of nature and the philosophy of Transcendentalism. His so deceptively simple descriptions of nature and the depth of his thoughts on the spiritual implications of such nonhuman reality are the highwater mark of the contrary direction of this new American spirit. In the chapter "Where I Lived, and What I Lived For" Thoreau expresses his Taoist-like conception of the Emersonian "fundamental unity," the revelation, at its inception, of an awareness of universal subjectivity: "Every morning was a cheerful invitation to make my life of equal simplicity, and I may say innocence, with Nature herself."[148]

The reason we must turn to nature as a mirror of our own spirituality is that the Puritan ethos of the pursuit of the external thing has supressed that spirituality in its purist form. Addressing the enormity of this problem at a time when the problem was first seriously being recognized by Emerson and others, Thoreau, much like William Blake, created an extended metaphor that compares this Puritan ethos to sleep. Thoreau called for a revolution of spirit to wake men from this sleep. He predicated this revolution, which engenders a child-like openness to the potentiality of experience, upon an Emersonian exchange with nature, not upon commerce: "To him whose elastic and vigorous thought keeps pace with the sun, the day is perpetual morning. It matters not what the clocks say or the attitudes and labors of men."[149] Yet Thoreau was aware that he was almost alone in his understanding of the need for such a rev-

olution because most men were aware of no other consciousness than
that of the Puritan:

The millions are awake enough for physical labor; but only one in a million is
awake enough for effective intellectual exertion, only one in a hundred millions
to a poetic or a divine life. To be awake is to be alive. I have never met a man
who was quite awake. How could I have looked him in the face?

We must learn to reawaken and keep ourselves awake, not by mechanical aids,
but by an infinite expectation of the dawn, which does not forsake us in our
soundest sleep.[150]

Versions of North American haibun, in their profoundest form, are
records of such awakenings.

Notes

A version of this introduction appeared as "North American Versions of Haibun" in three consecutive installments of *Modern Haiku* (Winter–Spring 1997, Summer 1997, Fall 1997).

1. *Haiku Moment: An Anthology of Contemporary North American Haiku*, ed. by Bruce Ross (Boston: Charles E. Tuttle Co., Inc., 1993), xii–xiii.
2. See Bruce Ross, "Refiguring Nature: Tropes of Estrangement in Contemporary American Poetry," *Analecta Husserliana* XXXVII (1991), 299–311.
3. K. Masuda, *Kenkyusha's New Pocket Japanese–English Dictionary* (Tokyo: Kenkyusha, n.d.), 239.
4. *The Princeton Companion to Classical Japanese Literature*, ed. by Earl Miner, Hiroaki Odagiri, and Robert E. Morrell (Princeton: Princeton University Press, 1985), 275.
5. See William J. Higginson, *The Haiku Handbook* (New York: McGraw-Hill, 1985), 288; Earl Miner, *Japanese Linked Poetry* (Princeton: Princeton University Press, 1979), 361; *From the Country of the Eight Islands, An Anthology of Japanese Poetry*, ed. by Hiroaki Sato and Burton Watson (New York: Columbia University Press, 1986), 624; and Makoto Ueda, *The Master Haiku Poet Matsuo Bashō* (Tokyo: Kodansha, 1982), 112.
6. Haiku Society of America, "Draft Definitions Submitted for Member Comment" (January 1994), 2.
7. Higginson, *Haiku Handbook*, 67.
8. "Haibun," *Point Judith Light* II:2 (1993), 8.
9. By Gary Snyder, from *Earth House Hold*. Copyright © 1969 by Gary Snyder. Reprinted by permission of New Directions Publishing Corp.
10. Ueda, *Master Haiku Poet Matsuo Bashō*, 123–124.

11. Snyder, *Earth House Hold*, 8, 11.

12. Jack Kerouac, *The Dharma Bums* (New York: Signet, 1958), 48.

13. Snyder, *Earth House Hold*, 4.

14. Jack Kerouac, *Desolation Angels* (New York: Bantam, 1965), 75.

15. Ibid., 76.

16. Ibid., 77.

17. Ibid.

18. Ibid., 91.

19. Ibid.

20. Rod Willmot, *Ribs of Dragonfly* (Windsor, Ontario: Black Moss, 1984), 41.

21. Ibid., 62.

22. Ibid., 10.

23. Ibid., 8–9.

24. Ibid., 11.

25. Ibid., 69.

26. Ibid., 73.

27. Vincent Tripi, *Haiku Pond: A trace of the trail...and Thoreau* (San Francisco: Vide, 1987), *xiii*.

28. Ibid., *xiv*.

29. Ibid., 1.

30. Ibid.

31. Ibid., 23.

32. Ibid..

33. Ibid.

34. Ibid., 25.

35. Ibid.

36. Ibid., 57.

37. Ibid., 58.

38. Ibid., 59.

39. Ibid.

40. Hal Roth, "Winter Haibun," *Modern Haiku* XXIII:2 (1992), 57.

41. Dennis Kalkbrenner, "Lake Superior," *Modern Haiku* XXIV:1 (1993), 56.

42. J. P. Trammell, "Sunset on Cadillac Mountain," *Modern Haiku* XXIV:1 (1993), 59.

43. Ibid.

44. G. R. Simser, "Water Spider," *Modern Haiku* XXV:1 (1994), 48.

45. Ibid.

46. Ibid.

47. Liz Fenn, "No Monkey Business," *Point Judith Light* II:2 (1993), 9.

48. Personal letter, April 27, 1993.

49. Dave Sutter, "Italia: Quattrocento/Ventecento," *Frogpond* XVI:1 (1993), 41.

50. J. P. Trammell, "The Temple of the Snail," *Modern Haiku* XXV:1 (1994), 45–46.

51. Leatrice Lifshitz, "Far From Home," *Modern Haiku* XXIV:1 (1993), 60.

52. Ibid., 61.

53. Ibid.

54. Robert Spiess, *Five Caribbean Haibun* (Madison, Wisc.: Wells, 1972), 51.

55. Ibid., 55.

56. Tom Lynch, *Rain Drips from the Trees: Haibun along the Trans–Canadian Highway* (733 N Raymond Street, Las Cruces, NM 88005), 34.

57. Ibid., 35.

58. Ibid., 27.

59. Ibid., 59.

60. Ibid., 32.

61. Ibid., 5.

62. Ibid., 14.

63. Ibid., 10, 13.

64. Ibid., 10.

65. Ibid., 24.

66. Ibid., 25.

67. Ibid., 26.

68. Penny Harter, *At the Zendō* (Santa Fe, N.M.: From Here, 1993), 21.

69. Ibid., 24.

70. Ibid., 25.

71. Ibid., 25–26.

72. Ibid., 29–30.

73. William J. Higginson and Penny Harter, *Met on the Road: A Transcontinental Haiku Journey* (Foster City, Calif.: Press Here, 1993), 11.

74. Ibid., 13.

75. Ibid., 19.

76. Ibid., 17.

77. Ibid., 24.

78. Ibid., 31.

79. Ibid., 21.

80. Brent Partridge, *Road through the Stars* (unpublished), 1.

81. Ibid., 9.

82. Ibid., 17.

83. Ibid., 2.

84. Ibid., 7.

85. Ibid., 2.

86. Ibid., 13.

87. Ibid., 10.

88. Ibid., 12.

89. Ibid., 16.

90. Ibid., 18.

91. Ibid.

92. Ibid.

93. Personal letter, April 27, 1993.

94. Frank Trotman, "Early Morning," *Brussels Sprout* IX:3 (1992), 31.

95. Ibid.

96. Cor van den Heuvel, "Curbstones," *Modern Haiku* XXIII:2 (1992), 58.

97. Ibid.

98. Ibid., 59.

99. Christopher Herold, "Scarecrows," *Frogpond* XV:2 (1992), 42.

100. Ibid., 43.

101. Patrick Frank, "Return to Springfield: Urban Haibun," *Point Judith Light* II:3 (1993), 12.

102. Liz Fenn, "Big Bucks on Tug Hill," *Modern Haiku* XXIV:2 (1993), 90.

103. Ibid.

104. Cathy Drinkwater Better, "Father-in-Law," *Point Judith Light* II:3 (1993), 12.

105. Rich Youmans, "Sunday Visits," *Frogpond* XVII:3 (1994), 26.

106. Ibid.

107. Tom Tico, "Bird Song and Bare Branches," *Frogpond* XIV:4 (1991), 22.

108. Ibid., 25.

109. Tom Tico, "In the Spirit of the Samurai," *Frogpond* XVI:2 (1992), 45.

110. Tom Tico, "Reaching for the Rain," *Frogpond* XV:1 (1992), 38.

111. Patricia Neubauer, "The Goldfish Vendor," *Modern Haiku* XXIV:2 (1993), 89.

112. Ibid.

113. Patricia Neubauer, "Primavera," *Modern Haiku* XXV:1 (1994), 30.

114. Kerouac, *The Dharma Bums*, 48.

115. Cor van den Heuvel, *A Boy's Seasons,* in *Modern Haiku* XXIV:3 (1993), 75.

116. Ibid., 76.

117. Ibid., 77.

118. Ibid., 77–78.

119. Ibid., 82.

120. Ibid., 79.

121. Ibid., XXV:1 (1994), 41.

122. Ibid., 35.

123. Tom Clausen, *Going to Grandma's* (unpublished), 3.

124. Ibid., 2.

125. Ibid., 3.

126. Tom Clausen, "New Sneakers," *Brussels Sprout* XI:1 (1994), 24.

127. Ibid., 26.

128. Tom Clausen, "Before School," *Point Judith Light* II:3 (1993), 12.

129. Ibid.

130. Ibid.

131. Bruce Ross, "Aglow," *Modern Haiku* XXV:2 (1994), 46.

132. Ibid.

133. Ibid.

134. Ibid.

135. Rich Youmans, "For My Wife on Our First Anniversary," *Brussels Sprout* XI:3 (1994), 15.

136. Ibid.

137. Ibid.

138. Ibid.

139. William M. Ramsey, "Gurdjieff, Zen, and Meher Baba," *Modern Haiku* XXV:3 (1994), 37.

140. Ibid., 38.

141. Ibid.

142. Ibid.

143. Ibid.

144. Ibid.

145. Ibid.

146. Chong Sun Kim, "Alienation and the Tao," *Point Judith Light* III:1 (1994), 14.

147. Ibid., 14–15.

148. Henry David Thoreau, *Walden and Civil Disobedience* (New York: Penguin, 1983), 132.

149. Ibid., 134.

150. Ibid.

Journey
to the Interior

Before School

He's going to kindergarten in two weeks. The school was holding a pre-event at the playground for parents and children to mingle and get to know each other. We had gotten a notice about it a week or so ago.

I got home from work at twenty-five after five. My bike ride home had been a pleasant passage; noticing the sky and its scattered wispy clouds streaking way off, feeling the reassurance of once again making my way through such a long, long familiar space. I had fixed my arrival home on going for a refreshing end of the day swim.... It had been around ninety degrees at work. You get an idea, a vision and you can see how life just flows to meet that moment. Sometimes.

In the door my wife mentions the playground thing. She says it's tonight, I say fine, you both go right ahead. She replies she's tired, too tired to go, a headache too. I sense the old test of self once again rearing its ugly head in mine, as it has thousands of times before and no doubt it will a good thousand times to come. The stand-off lasted all of ten tense minutes and then I said okay let's go Casey and sneakers on we let the screen door slap between us.

The playground...the school, the same one I went to over thirty years earlier, yet somehow heading there had no hold on my imagination or fancy. Instead a slight sullenness and dread filled me at having to make an appearance for some other adults who I feared would be less able than me to honestly confront how hard it is to be...a parent. No doubt I'm having a time pulling it off and here was a test of my being...a parent. School for Casey was going to begin my need to meet head-on just what it is other parents are doing or more realistically what am I doing and does the job measure up on a public yardstick.

Well we get there and quite by surprise no one else is there. We wait and wait, Casey plays, I chase him around. We enjoy the space, the peace and quiet, the setting down day…must be she got the time or week or day…something…

> before school
> about the empty playground
> a monarch

Birds

Both my parents despised guns and people using them so it was no small triumph when I ended up with my very own BB gun when I was in sixth grade. Of course I was restricted in how I could use it but proudly carried it about in the fields and woods behind our house. There was a feeling of connection to every soldier and hunter although I mostly shot at cans, trees, or little paper bull's-eye targets. Once along our brook I spotted a redheaded woodpecker way up on a dead elm tree. It peered down at me motionless. In a cruel moment of unclear curiosity I aimed up and pulled the trigger. The BB, totally against gravity, seemed to hit, puff, right in the chest, without any effect. I gazed up, it gazed down. It was a solemn-sad-satori to feel the hollowness of what I had done. I was relieved and glad when the woodpecker flew away. I had not a bit of hunter in my heart and vowed I would not aim at anything alive ever again.

My father had grown up a bird lover and had always wanted to become an ornithologist. We had bird feeders and bird houses all around our yard, including a two-tier, sixteen-hole deluxe purple martin house on a high pole in our back yard. Annually there was the problem of starlings finding the martin house to be an ideal nesting site and out-competing the martins for these spaces. This starling versus martin debacle caused my father no small amount of consternation. I was astonished when my father approached me about using my new BB gun to discourage the starling invasion. He didn't want me to actually shoot the starlings but suggested I shoot near them or hit the side of the martin house when starlings attempted to land. I was offered a vague bounty to spend time shooting from a second floor window, selectively trying to scare starlings away while protecting the nesting work of martins. There was a bizarre novelty to be shooting out from our house at my father's bird house yet above that I remember wondering what on earth was I doing and thinking why is one bird better than another.

Today on my bicycle ride home from work on a stretch of walkway an elderly woman yelled to me as I was passing, "I found out what kind of birds they are!" Her manner indicated clearly she mistook me to be someone she had previously discussed this with. I stopped, puzzled at what she meant and now with my full attention she said again, "I found out what kind of birds are in our bird house." I said "Oh, what are they?" She said disgustedly, "They're starlings, and we so wanted flickers!"

> the garden
> he tended so caringly...
> all gone to weeds

New Sneakers

When our five-and-a-half-year-old son, Casey, began a campaign for new sneakers it awakened in me the memories of my own childhood love affair with the nearly annual new pair. For a child there is an extra-sensory exhilaration that comes from having one's feet laced into a springy new pair of sneakers.

Casey had been pleading for weeks for a new pair of Nikes. At first I was mildly disturbed that he was brand and style conscious at only five. After all, my childhood sneakers had been plain canvas Skippys bought at five-and-dime stores, and they had been absolutely captivating to me. Furthermore, as an adult I've never warmed up to the large, clumpy, light-up-glaring barges that so many kids adore today. Oh well, my doubts were soon replaced by vicarious enjoyment of his pleasure with his new Nikes. He had me hold them, inspect their tread and note each and every feature of their design.

Watching Casey run, jump, skip and thoroughly exalt about in his new shoes made it perfectly clear he was proud, enthused and inspired by the collaboration of his dream come true in the form of two pieces of rubber life attached to his feet. I was instructed to look closely at the first grass stains and the first mud in the tread and in general much focus that first day was placed firmly on his embellished feet! I knew they would get old like many prized toys past their peak of charm, yet I'll never forget that night when still brand-new these sneakers were the magic of a young heart and mind.

five-year-old snuggles
his new sneakers
in bed

The Near and Far

Utah summer, due west through sunstruck sagebrush. Flat. Now finally, where one steer wanders, the road starts swirling downward past an old corral, pearl-gray, smooth. The road drops, drops, deep into a canyon, a place of sometimes water. Cottonwoods, green, rooted deep.

Quiet here in the dappled shade. Sheltered. On the cliff top, pinyon and sage, but here

> beneath white sandstone
> whorled down by wind
> in dinosaur eons
> a sheltering cliff—
>   petroglyphs

Petroglyphs pecked through dark desert varnish into red Kayenta sandstone. A holy place.

Newspaper Rock State Historical Monument, 1961. Forbidding fence, flagstones, nature trail with guide. All to help a holy place keep silence. A sign says we can't date petroglyphs, but this site seems to have been in use for 2,000 years—prehistory up to 1300 by various pueblo tribes—Fremont, Archaic, Basketmaker, etc. Navajo. It claims no one knows what these petroglyphs mean. What? The cliff reverberates with what they mean. Magic is what they mean.

Antlered deer pecked in rock beside horned dancers. Hunting magic. Above them, giant feathered triangles—

　　　　　feathered triangles
　　　　　dance above the ancients
　　　　　Shamans

And crosses. Crosses within circles, a cross on mounded earth. All jumbled in space and time. But magic. Magic that can be read. Magic that can be felt in the marrow of the bones.

Over to the right, tracks, large and small. Not mother and child, but near and far, in place and in time. Deer, bear, raccoon, and rabbit. Man. All tracking skyward to the Great Father. Pictures of souls are pecked here too: bison, mountain sheep, lizards. A long line of deer walking toward a hunter on horseback: Willingly I give my soul unto your care, oh my brother, for your need.

　　　　　One handprint, one only:
　　　　　I, man,
　　　　　I made this magic

Down below, over to the side, a longhorn steer pounded into rock stampedes. A wagon wheel and a longhorn steer: cowboys—vaqueros— bringing their crosses to the rock. Under the highest one, ladder-high, under its blessing, a name and date in a firm, fine draftsman's hand: J. P. Gonsalez 6/3/1902. Another pilgrim coming by chance or by intent crudely pecked his name beneath: C. D. Gonsales 6/3/54.

Others came: NA and MH, JB and LF, for holy places pull men to them out of the emptiness. Peace marchers came, making their sign here, their circle with its walking Y. Before the State of Utah stepped in and planted this iron fence between the hand and the rock.

　　　　　but each still speaks
　　　　　out of the jumbled near and far
　　　　　out of the now and then

Turtle

Yesterday, I was at a pow-wow. Today, even though I'm not a Native, a gladiolus juts out of the ground with multiple buds, like a spear with many feathers that points the way to the heavens.

Thirty years ago, I had a turtle. I captured him and kept him in a box. I gave him food and water and thought he would love me and stay in my house. But the turtle wouldn't eat. Finally, my father, who had said it was okay to keep the turtle, told me I had to let him go.

My father didn't make me do this right away. I didn't want to let the turtle go because I loved him. He seemed very old and very wise. He most likely was older than me. I thought the turtle had something great to tell me.

When my parents and I were on our way to go to the store, my father told me I had to put the turtle back where I found him. I placed him back under the very same bush. The turtle seemed in no great hurry to leave. I took this as a sign that the turtle loved me and would stay. Its problem was the box, not me. Now that the turtle was outside, he would choose to stay.

As we left in the car, my father thought that this was not true. The turtle will leave, he said. No, I told him. When we returned home, I looked under the bush. The turtle was gone. I looked under other bushes, then the yard, then the street. No turtle. I cried, thinking the turtle didn't love me, that he had nothing to say to me after all.

friend gone
the silence
of untouched water

Yesterday I met an Iroquois man who told me that the earth was created on the back of a giant snapping turtle. The snapping turtle had twenty-eight plates on its underside. There are twenty-eight days between moons. There are thirteen plates on the turtle's back— thirteen moons in a year, thirteen tectonic plates on the earth.

The Iroquois prophesied that, though they would be driven nearly to extinction, their way of life would form the laws that govern the entire earth and bring all the races together in peace. They prophesied that the trees would die from the top down. Acid rain has proven this prophecy true. They prophesied that all nations would come together as one on Iroquois land. The U.N. has proven this prophecy true.

Today, the spear-like flower points to the sky. Most of my race has become aware that the earth is not a pet we can keep in a box and cultivate the way we want. The animals will all die. The earth herself will not speak to us. I remember you, turtle.

hearing what you said
thirty years
after you said it

Haibun for Dennis: December 12, 1994

I needed to get out of the house. The obscenity of objects bare of him. At Blue Hill, the cliffs near the main path were covered with a thin sheet of ice where bluish lichen and patches of soaked moss showed through. Suddenly I noticed the intermittent water droplets between ice and rock, corpuscle-like black shapes. It was like looking at the movement of blood under a microscope. Somehow the horizontal pull of the pattern kept the submerged waterfall in unearthly suspension as all across the broad rock face the globes of water came curvetting down the six or seven inches before catching in the comb of ice, flexing between surfaces, and falling.... Back at the front door it was as if I looked again through a window of ice.

> in the empty house
> prism light from the window
> soaks the woodwork

The Red

The cat is suddenly in my face licking the tip of my nose. In an odd effusive spell he marches across my keyboard, knocks over paper and pens, wraps his tail around the arm of my halogen light. I'm feeling you come through him; a chill across my skin. He looks directly in my eyes and keeps on looking, the reddish markings underneath the gray and black around his nose and mouth blur in the blue light of the computer screen. Lying down on the bedroom floor, the whole house tips upside down as if awkwardly gauged stairs led down hallway to bathroom, then again into the shower. I get up, walk to the bathroom, begin opening the drawers. In the third: Q-Tips, Visine, nail clippers, #15 sun screen...

an old razor...

For a moment the reddish fur of the cocker, the reddish grain of the hardwood floor, a prism edge along the wainscoting at the red/orange band of the spectrum glow like embers and I remember that first autumn falling in love, the red flushed through everything like a wound plunged underneath a faucet. Then it drains in a breath. The cat is just "the cat" wanting to be fed.

> a year from your death
> bright red bristles of your beard
> in an old razor

Return to Springfield: Urban Haibun

Saturday I returned to Springfield with my wife. She dropped me off at the ghetto court across from Burger King where I used to play. Despite the city's long-standing and well-publicized "urban renewal" program, the physical condition of the court and surrounding area are badly deteriorated:

> back to the city—
> glass litters
> the ground

The court itself, where neighborhood kids are supposed to go to stay out of trouble and play, is a disgrace. The flotsam and jetsam of urban life have been discarded at the court's perimeter.

> cigarette butts
> everywhere beside
> the ghetto court

> the shattered pieces
> of a transistor
> radio

I have returned, unemployed, to a city I abandoned more than a year ago, seduced by the promise of a well-paying job in coastal Rhode Island. The job fell through, so my wife and I are sort of stranded. Despite its seemingly intractable problems, we miss Springfield, and if we found jobs in the area would immediately return. I guess I am an anomaly, a Southerner who, after more than a decade living in New

England, has grown fond of a Northern city, a white man who feels more comfortable in a black neighborhood than he does in a largely Caucasian resort community.

I fantasize that if I return, I will become involved in helping to generate "urban renewal" at a genuine grass roots level. There is plenty of work to be done:

> graffiti scrawled
> on a broken green
> > fence
>
> no screens
> on windows
> of the tenement

I "shoot around" at the one goal that is remaining, becoming immersed in the internal rhythm of my solitary game. Like most basketball players, I have devised a system for working out, when no one else is around. I begin to lose track of time and also become unaware of the immediate surroundings, so I am surprised to discover that a black man of about my age, and dressed like me in raggedy clothes, has joined me on the court. He begins by expressing outrage at the condition of the area—voicing my internal perception—and proceeds to tell me that he left Springfield for East Providence, Rhode Island several years ago, but has children here, misses Springfield, and wants in the worst way to come back. But he is unemployed.

The parallels between us are more than striking. It seems uncanny that we have met this way, and are engaged in this sort of conversation. His name is Bartley; we shake hands, and he asks if he can shoot around with me for a while. Of course I say yes, and we continue to talk about various things, like the recent death of Reggie Lewis.

Bartley says, "My people told me not to give up my job and leave, but just like Reggie, I got a second opinion. I don't know what it is about Rhode Island, I just can't get used to it. Springfield still feels like home. If I could find a job, I'd move back in a second."

I told him I am in the same boat. We talked more about Reggie, about how he helped so many kids. He was one of those athletes who involves himself in the community. And we continued to shoot. I was hitting my long bombs. He seemed impressed. He also seemed to be in a somewhat weakened physical condition, as if he were sick, or just worn down. We played for about half an hour but the heat started to get to me, so we shook hands, and I retired to Burger King, to drink coffee and read. We parted with the words, "If we both come back to Springfield, we'll probably see each other again."

I felt I had made a friend.

As I reflect on this whole experience, the double image that pops into my mind is as follows:

> greenery entwined
> in a chain-link fence
>
> wild flowers growing
> out of cracks
> in the cement

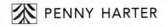

At Home

November 8, 1988 (HSA weekend at Spring Lake, NJ): It has been gathering, coming together—singing, poems, teaching, the desire to heal person and planet—the talents converging. Last night, the detachment from the party—at it, but not of it; the pull of the waves. Being washed clean by the wind, scudding gray clouds, rain, walking on the beach—I wake up pre-dawn with a sense of my whole life scrolling before me—not in word or image so much as texture or weight, or shape—like a vast coastline, the rhythm of the waves.

I write this so that I won't forget, not because the words matter. A glorious walk on the beach, an hour and a half, blazing blue sky, balmy November day, wind, gulls—so much in the moment—then packing, the train ride north.

Driving home from the station, things are cut-out, separate, like sliding by the train window.

Later, Home (Scotch Plains, NJ): Sorting to settle in, panpipes on tape, wind, sunlight outside through the transparency of yellow leaves, drifting near sleep, waking, sitting to begin to meditate—window sun wind music leaves—at once tears rolling down my cheeks, *knowing* we are only this, only precisely what we are doing at any given moment, no more; we are as transparent as the leaf in sunlight. Nothing matters because nothing exists. Our houses are just paper boxes blown down around us—our bodies are just paper bags blown in around us. Inside we go out and up—we are nothing except everything else. I truly don't know who, better yet *what* I am, what *we* are, all of us peopling, infinite variety, yet all the same, since I (we) don't exist except in the moment, constantly changing. I cannot die since I am not born but only passing through like a gust of wind shaking a clutch of leaves and moving on.

And I can't stop the tears, see everything so separate and unified simultaneously—I feel so much slower. Writing doesn't even matter, lovers don't matter, parent and child, husband and wife, living and dying—*all the same.*

To try to hold on to this—violation. To be unable to let go of this—inevitable. To let go of it all—of course. And even this experience is nothing!

Energy=love=light=wind of luminous, nameless particles in us all. Blowing and blowing always.

Words can't do it now.

> bare in winter
> green in summer—
> where is the tree now?

A Weekend at Dai Bosatsu Zendō

September 1987

Morning, sky blue and clear, wind crisp and cool, the first autumnal weather after a long muggy summer. We pick up Tadashi and John outside Grand Central Station, then leave New York City over the George Washington Bridge to drive up the Palisades Interstate Parkway, heading for the Catskills.

We stop at a scenic overlook with a small restaurant/snack bar. After eating, we walk to the lookout over the Hudson. Downriver on the opposite bank the city thrusts spires into the morning sky. Here, poison ivy, rocks, a few candy wrappers.

Resuming the journey...

> on the way to the zendō
> the thump, thump, thumping
> of a nail in our tire

on the drive across the border into New York State. We find an open gas station, hoping not to lose too much time.

> fixing our flat
> the mechanic tells us
> of his baby daughter

We climb now into the mountains, a profusion of goldenrod and purple aster in fields by the roadside.

> autumn morning—
> the smell of a recent fire
> in these wet woods

A tape of shakuhachi music fills the car with melody. Sky. Drifting clouds. We stop at a local diner in Livingston Manor to stretch our legs.

> in front of the diner
> bending over the garden
> Tadashi names each flower

Inside we have a snack and use the bathroom.

> She asks me for a tampon
> the girl "in a car with three guys"
> on her way to New York

Up the narrow road then, following signs for the zendō. Climbing and winding through the woods, we drive along beside a brook that reflects the startling blue of the sky as it bubbles over rocks.

> sitting among
> pine roots by the brook—
> stone Buddha

Some leaves flash red. Twice, deer leap across the road in front of us. I feel the energy, the unknown waiting on the mountain-top.

Turning in at the gates to the zendō, we begin the two-mile approach. A dirt road rises through forest; we glimpse abandoned orchards, distant vegetable rows in clearings through the trees. Just before crossing the rattling wooden bridge over the brook to turn into the driveway, we see Bashō's haiku carved into a polished stone:

> along this way
> goes no one
> this autumn evening

Suddenly, Dai Bosatsu Zendō, white walls, graceful roof, set in a clearing on a forested slope that descends to the lake.

After unloading bags at the door, we drive back to a grassy area by the woodshed to park. A sign warns to check brake lines and hoses when leaving; porcupines sometimes chew them. Walking back up the driveway to the zendō in the chilly air, we see the shimmer of water far down through the trees.

We take off shoes to leave them on a shelf in the shoe-room near the door. Then, barefoot, to our room. Simple and spare, tatami mats, futon, floor bare and polished, two windows.

Before supper we put on shoes again, descend through trees to the lake. Inscribed on a wooden plaque mounted on a tree at the water's edge, an anonymous verse:

> ten years searching in the deep forest—
> now great laughter
> at the edge of the lake

I stand quietly by the water. Fish leap from the surface, ripples touching.

> autumn wind
> rippling the water,
> my hair

> far off
> among the fallen trees—
> footsteps

We go in to supper, past the young nun with shaved head beating the dinner gong. Delicious homemade lentil soup, salad, fresh baked warm bread. The group sits on cushions around low tables.

Later, those who wish to rise at 5 A.M. the next day for morning services and *zazen* (sitting meditation) receive instructions in the meditation hall. The faint smell of sandalwood. A candle flickers before the Buddha at the altar. Sliding shōji screens. Our names above the cushions. And then to bed.

first night
no soft place
for tender bones

Before sunrise the next morning, a bell rings in the hallway outside the room. I pull on a sweater, use the bathroom, brush hair into a ponytail. Then I join the others walking silently toward the meeting place—the corridor around the meditation hall. At the opening to the hall a monk in full lotus sits, candlelight flickering on his dark robe, shaved head. He has always been there.

We line up, still silent, for exercise. Following the head monk we fast-walk, then run around the corridor. One more round. And then another. Heart pounding, into the morning service. Chanting the sutras, louder, faster, louder still, to drumbeat.

first morning service—
following the sutras
without my glasses

After an hour of chanting, spirit and body strangely stirred by the Heart Sutra, I feel a deep recognition. Back into the meditation hall to sit, facing the shōji and half a square of window in the corridor, looking out onto a slope...

> dawn light
> mist in the grass,
> wildflowers

I close my eyes to stay with counting breaths—breathing. Wooden sticks clatter rhythmically. Random bells. At first mind noisy.

> stomach growling
> my neighbor's?
> my own?

At the gong we rise to walk for ten silent minutes, through the corridor and then outside along the wooden deck around the inner courtyard, inside again, down the still dark hallway by the rooms, and back into the meditation hall.

> silent walking
> in the zendō hallway—
> a window!

> *kinhin*
> my lover's bare feet
> blue-veined

Another half hour of zazen. No time passes, and at the gong my eyes start open to see each thing distinct, luminous, itself.

after meditation
one leaf settles
into the grass

sunrise—
tree trunks
dividing mist

Chanting, we file in, to a silent breakfast. Unfolding the cloth that covers the chopsticks and nested lacquer bowls we carried from the meditation hall, we place chopsticks on our right, tips angled off the table's edge, and separate the bowls, all following last night's instructions.

just oatmeal in the bowl—
oatmeal glistening
in the bowl

I add peanuts and raisins, homemade maple syrup, warm milk, then slide each serving dish down the long table to the others. All place bits of grain on the breadboard, part of the offering brought to the small altar on the mantle. Later to be given to the birds. Nothing wasted here.

silent breakfast—
pegs in the floor
of the dining hall

At meal's end, the garbage crock for orange skins, and the pot of hot water. I fill my large bowl. Fingers wash chopsticks and then the bowls. I dry each with the small white cotton towel after pouring the slop water from the middle bowl into the garbage crock and drinking the last sip before final wiping. Is all this in the correct order? It doesn't matter right now. I stack and wrap bowls, chopsticks, and cloth to return them to the meditation hall, place them on the floor behind the cushions until the next morning.

At 9 A.M. we assemble for the first haiku workshop. The group, most of whom rose early for service and zazen, is joyful and openly friendly to one another. Bill talks about the history of haiku and gives many fine contemporary examples. All write haiku and share.

Lunch. Vegetarian casserole, fresh bread, home-grown salad. At 2 P.M. I speak on "Why I Write Haiku." Then everyone is turned loose to wander the grounds for an hour, writing.

> on the same stalk
> milkweed blossom
> milkweed pod
>
> the two fawns
> seeing me, bolt away
> the doe foraging
>
> —Bill

Many come back with strong pieces, wanting to share.

Late afternoon. Apple-picking time. We jump into the old stake truck. I climb up into the cab.

> on the truck seat
> a garden glove
> holds flowering herbs

Gently, I lift the glove for Margaret to carry into the kitchen along with the plastic bag of still-muddy squash and carrots. Then we bounce and rattle down the mountain. Clark is driving, and others in back call out warnings for low-hanging branches. Shouts and laughter.

Arriving, we jump out into the orchard to begin filling baskets and crates. I find a long stick to knock down ripe apples. How tightly they hold on. Among the fallen apples deer droppings. Tadashi climbs the trees, shaking a rain of half-ripe apples into the tall grass. We cannot find all of them, feel glad to leave some for the deer. Finally, we lug overflowing baskets and crates back to the truck.

> apple basket full
> she still runs back
> for that red one

At night, Tadashi gives a talk on *renku*; then groups form and begin to write. Clark, Bill, Tadashi, John and I help at each table. Beer, sake, popcorn and fellowship smooth the way. And then to sleep, much too late. I lie quietly, remembering the presence in the corner of the dining hall:

> evening meditation
> the jade plant sits
> next to its reflection

Sunday morning, we rise again for service and meditation. Then breakfast, and meeting. Clark gives a clear-water talk on the non-relationship between haiku and Zen. Then Bugyō, vice-abbot, speaks on "Who Is the Poet?"

> bouncing a ball
> on the wooden table
> Bugyō talks

Smiling. Understanding. No words. A few moments later:

>	signing my name
>	in the book I wrote
>	the pen runs out of ink

Lunch. Back to the room to pack. Dropping the bags by the door. Before leaving, we pay homage at Sōen Roshi's grave.

>	climbing to the stupa—
>	not stepping on
>	the red salamander

Standing before the polished stone, I feel the peace of the grassy rise. We come down again to Bashō's poem:

>	along this way
>	goes no one
>	this autumn evening

We load the car, hug and kiss one another good-bye. Time to leave the zendō (the porcupines have not chewed brake lines or hoses). Non-attachment. Looking back. A fine rain begins as we drive down the mountain. The sky in the brook, gray.

>	among the trees
>	somewhere rain falling
>	on the doe's back

>	coming down
>	so many more leaves
>	have turned

Bright All

It is a cold morning, and I am up with the first light, loading the stove with split oak. Snow has fallen throughout the night, continues to fall, and frost blossoms on the inside of the single-pane windows. The gray of the morning is diffuse, depthless. The whole world recedes evenly, without shadow or interruption.

I know where the river should wander, where the mountain ought to rise up, but the truth today is that there is no river, no mountain. It would be easy to imagine, were it not for the solidity of this encompassing house, that somehow overnight I had been translated to some other state.

Over a breakfast of grape nuts and dried fruit, I muse on my true solitude here, this morning, as sole as Adam in his garden before Eve and the fall. (The dog's head-shaking yawn disabuses me of this idea, and, good animal that he is, he moves a couple paces closer to the woodstove.) But I will insist upon my general impression: if the particulars of my situation fail to bear it out, still do I live in paradise—the word, derived from old Greek and Arabic sources, means "orchard," and suggests a place of ordered bounty—not only because of the providence of this land, but for the fecundity of mind possible here. All wandering cultures speak of such a place as this, where pear and cherry, fig and quince, might be plucked with ease and eaten at leisure; but even more, a place where one might be most at ease, most fruitful. And what is this ease but a getting by heart of the way home? A knowing of the land, and one's place in and on it? Paradise is being at home where you live.

walking in
the orchard   suddenly
its plan

Above, the storm abates, though the day remains sealed by twi-light. Clouds, the color of iron and the breadth of the sky, don't move. It is virtually impossible to tell earth from sky, near from far, but I know where to look.

Below, the swale down to the river deepens to a huskier blue. A flock of crows, venturing out after the storm in search of food, follow it and disappear over the crest into the darkness. Their cries remain a long time with me.

Before me, I can differentiate the white hillock to the east from the grayer hulk of Blue Mountain which looms behind it. A female red fox, her flanks and back white with snow, suddenly appears at the top of the rise. The male, plangent voice howling, circles and mounts her—done in a moment—then pads across the meadow, nose held to the wind, while she lies down in the snow.

Behind me, the pines darken against the horizon. Chickadees, somewhere sheltered through the storm, drop down from the lowest branches and beak through the snow. Their hop and flutter leaves clear tracks and soft brush marks in the deep powder.

To the right, the craggy limbs of the apple trees have thrown off their snow-cover, exposing their black gnarl to view. Three deer move out of the south woods, root up some drops from beneath the snow cover, begin to nibble. The frontmost, a large buck, finds something of interest in the middle distance, stares at it for long moments.

To the left, along the fire road, my nearest human neighbor appears, a mere speck of red wool against the white landscape. Above the pines which hide his dwelling rises the white stream of smoke which fragrances my winter walks, and which tells me he is well. The sharp bark of his axe reports a moment later.

The dog ambles over, places his muzzle on my left thigh. The map of Six Directions takes shape, stretches out again in space and time, becomes the place where I live, this place, my home.

> clear here
> but haze to the east,
> haze to the west

The Order of Stars

All summer long I share this river with the various migrant species that come to shelter and feed in its bounteous arms: Canada geese and sandhill cranes, upland beavers and lowland muskrat, fleet trout and wallowing carp; and, most seasonally, other human beings as well. With them I exchange small talk about crops and crappies, great blues and boats, the weather and the World Series. For a few months the most notable objects on the water are bright-colored fiberglass craft powered by noisy engines churning through the steady clear currents. Along the shore, silver trailers with out-of-state plates and mud-splattered pick-ups beside orange tents pop up in the flood plain. Smoky fires and loud talk ride the wind.

> calm evening
> the ballgame comes play-by-play
> across the water

When autumn appears, and the waters cool, first week-days, then all days, find the river devoid of men. It is at this time, when the river and I are alone, that I am most able to come to my senses, become most truly human. It is not that I do not enjoy the company of my fellow men. But their presence illustrates to me what a man is, while in their absence I am permitted to think on what a man can be, and to represent him well here among the wild and untutored, where there is no preference for things human. I am most able to shed the veneer of humanity, and simply be, a human animal amongst these other animals, a presence amidst their presences.

It is now, when the river is barren, that I am most forcibly struck by the solitariness of wild animals. How rare it is to see animals in the company of a species not their own. Bears do not traffic with deer, beavers give the muskrats a wide berth, and chipmunks dart away at the approach of a hare. Only the birds are excepted: upon the waters, intermingled, I espy mallards keeping company with Canada geese; the cranes and herons share the shingled bank; and the strong straight flights of the kingfisher are looped together by the barn swallows' arabesques.

The dog is happy enough on its own, quite apart from these deliberations. He races about for sheer joy, biting at the white water of the rapids, crackling leaves in haste to get from here to there for no purpose other than to do it.

cloudless sky
enjoying the dog
enjoying the river

Settling down for the evening on a mossy spot along the bank I am calmed by the river's steady flow. The water which I had passed over making my way here during the day now passes me by, bearing with it the traces of the many soils and landscapes it drains: Blue Ridge escarpment, Shenandoah Valley effluvium, Piedmont loess, mingle in these waters, are the mud and shine of its passing. Also flowing, the shine of the bright moon, the dim halo of stars about it, and, in the dark woods, my own shining being—

camping alone
the crackle of small sticks
in the fire

 DENNIS KALKBRENNER

Lake Superior

Wild roses near the pebble shore—their scent touches each cool stone and flows over clear water. Forgotten joy returns this misty summer morning—water holds vapors close until sunlight breaks the gentle bond of fog. A seagull screeches first light into sky. And then this breath taken in and exhaled wafts a rose bloom—a few petals fall on stone. Eyes grasp a perfect pebble: cast far off, it ripples the mirror lake—ruffles reflections still in sleep. Awake again all young dreams.

skipping stones
expanding echoes
disappear

Only a Stranger

Prologue

Always in autumn, when the backyard thins and the brittleness starts, I begin to think about mastering my grief. I bury the last chrysanthe-mums, plant a few bulbs for a softer season, and pray for a viable mercy. But still a stranger to myself, even now, in the middle of my life, I live with ghosts. I sit for hours with my head in my hands, listening to Scriabin, Bartók, and Liszt—drunk on sorrow, dreaming of home.

equinox:
cicada shells crumble
in the ivy

I

A chattering wind is bringing down the leaves. Remnants of bagworm and chestnut lie in the tangle. After long highway miles, I return to the mountains and the trees, to the old house that waits, tucked asleep, in an arm of the Adirondacks. Abandoned now, overgrown with bracken and vines, it sits sideways beside the creek, facing the forest instead of the road. After years of wandering through ruins I should have been prepared for this, but I never expected the tumbled chimney, the bro-ken windows, the foundation shifted and cracked, the piece of clap-board that hangs at the side of the house like a broken limb.

the empty mountain house
falling into
itself

II

Moonlight falls in fractions through dead bindweed, on milkweed pods that crack open and float away. In an upstairs window, a scrap of curtain moves aimlessly in and out of space. I should have come last summer, in sunlight, when the unbraided sky traveled in a thousand directions at once, a blue passageway flocked with white, or years ago when every season was spring with its risings and promise. But now, here and now, in the whirl of this brief sad season, I stand where I stood as a child, when life was liquid and thick, leaping in my wrists.

the autumn air textured
with woodsmoke and thistledown—
these memories

III

The air turns colder. Like a hard breath blown through the lips of God, it strikes a tamarack's stringed tongue. The tamarack trembles and moans. I begin to shiver. I can hear the creek as it stumbles over stones, a tired tenor losing its voice. In the open field next to the house, wild geese wake. In a sudden rush of wings, they remember the victory of flight.

between the stars
and the mountains,
a vee of migrating geese

IV

There is nothing to reclaim here. Everything changes but memory is holy—a difficult harmony. There is time for tomorrow—time to pity, to forgive, to love. Tonight I bless the past as I walk to the cusp of our hill where an old iron bridge stretches over the water. Somewhere on an edge of the night sky a small light begins to shine. It will gather momentum and fill the dark places. Forever is there, a glass bell that time rings through.

October mist—
only a stranger crossing
to the other side of the bridge

Chaco Canyon Haibun

There is a petroglyph on a small cliff in the desert about one and a half miles from the road. On cream-colored sandstone is a deep red painting of a star, a crescent moon, and the sun. It is thought to be a picture of the supernova of 1054. The rocks, sand and scraggly bushes are just about the same as 900 years ago. I stand alone in this vast expanse of desert and imagine an Anasazi Indian carefully painting this picture to record the fantastic event that he/she had witnessed. Now through this painting, here on this desert cliff, I can share that person's wonder of the cosmic forces that shape the universe and together across the centuries we marvel at the mystery.

> distant starlight
> falling on age-old rocks
> my hand casts a shadow

Arriving with the Tide

Saturday—Our First Day

I was hoping to get an early start but Jenny did not get up till late because she was out late with her friends last night. We begin our nine-day ride around 12:00 P.M.

On the ferry ride over to Kingston we discuss our plans for the trip. As we get off the ferry Jenny's bike falls as she tries getting on. It may take Jenny a little while to get used to the extra weight.

Just about ten miles up to the road Jenny's chain gets caught between her frame and her gears.

In the process of freeing her chain I manage to gouge my thumb on a part of her bike. I joke that we must look like two of the three stooges.

We make a stop at a great little greasy spoon in Discovery Bay called Fat Smitty's. After a good lunch break we start riding again. Taking lesser-used country roads is a welcome escape from the traffic of the highway.

the still bay
reflecting still
clouds

blue heron's wings
lightly brush the
reflecting water

We are still feeling energetic as we approach the South Sequim State Park, so we decide to ride on to Port Angeles and camp there. It is only another 15 miles and if I remember correctly it is mostly flat from here on.

Later...

We are taking a break at the Sequim Grocery Store. It turns out that the road is not flat at all. In fact it is almost all uphill with rolling hills. When we see a sign pointing the way to the Dungeness Spit Recreation area we both are happy to make it our new destination for the night.

When we arrive the campground is full!

We talk with the ranger who basically tells us to go find another campground. I decide to find a spot here anyway. Somewhere the ranger wouldn't see us.

We are now looking for a spot along a little-used hiking trail. When we find an opening in a fence leading to a farmer's field, I think to myself this is perfect. It's free, it's quiet and the ranger can't complain. Jenny felt uncomfortable just camping on someone's property so we walked over to the nearest house to ask permission. It's O.K.!!

We had soup for dinner and afterwards Jenny showed me an exercise to help awaken my kundalini.

above
my head a
cool breeze

under a
star-filled sky
frogs croaking

Sunday

I am boiling water for coffee and hot chocolate while I tune up and make a few adjustments on my bike.

While pouring water for her coffee, Jenny accidentally spills boiling water on her foot. I am concerned that it is a serious burn but, after putting some cold water and first aid ointment on it, it seems O.K.

We are taking the old Olympic Highway to Port Angeles. Some of the hills become quite steep as we approach town. I'm glad we didn't try to do this last night.

In Port Angeles Jenny gets a flat tire after riding over a deeply set sewer cover. I am able to fix the flat easily and in about ten minutes we are on our way again.

We stop for lunch at the Corner House Restaurant in Port Angeles "established in 1986." I am catching up on my journal writing and Jenny is working on her tax forms. It's hard to believe that she actually brought her tax paperwork along. We are planning to stop at the supermarket to get a couple of items and then we are on our way to Lake Crescent.

The ride around Lake Crescent is beautiful. We take a long break at Fairholm on the opposite end of Lake Crescent. We discuss the possibility of camping here or riding on to camp at state parks about 15–20 miles away, bringing us closer to the Hoh Rain Forest. We decide to go on.

Immediately we are faced with a very steep, very long uphill. But following this hill it is almost all gradual downhill. This is the most pleasant riding so far this trip. In fact it is so pleasant that we end up in Sappho, passing up our destination by almost two miles.

We head back and make camp just before it gets dark. We have lentil soup for dinner and then we sit by candlelight discussing relationships, philosophy, and Gina's moods.

Monday

We got up earlier this morning and got underway by almost 9:30. A half mile down the road I realize that I am riding with my cap on and that I had left my helmet back at camp. I told Jenny to go on and I'll catch up with her later. I went back and got my helmet and then started riding full speed ahead to catch up to Jenny.

I caught up to her in about twenty minutes. That was a great warm-up workout! We stop at the ranger station to get information about the road leading to the Hoh Rain Forest. After looking at a relief map of the area Jenny is confident that our ride into the Hoh Rain Forest will be relatively flat.

Later...

Now we are in Forks having a wonderful breakfast at the Rainy Cafe. Our plan is to ride into the Hoh Rain Forest today.

Later...

The ride into the Rain Forest is hilly with a couple of real killer hills. When we arrive at the campground it is almost full. We spend a long time going around in circles trying to decide which of the bad campsites left is the best. We finally decide to take one that is out in the open and breezy and thus less mosquito- and fly-infested.

Later...

I purchased wood from an old man and his wife selling firewood from the back of their pickup truck. Jenny is taking a nap right now and I'm getting ready to do the same.

Later still…

Jenny and I take the "Hall of Moss" trail and the "mini trail."

old man making a
phone call—his wife busily
brushing flies away

waving a white handkerchief
the flies think it's surrender

walking in the rain forest
not seeing any trees but
moss shaped like trees

And here's one Jenny wrote…

maple trees
dripping with moss
Hoh Rain Forest

Tuesday

The ride back to Highway 101 is much easier than the ride in yesterday.

The sky is overcast and it is starting to drizzle as we head south again on 101. The closer we get to Kalaloch Beach, which is our destination today, the darker the clouds and the harder it rains.

When we arrive at Kalaloch the first thing we do is have a good meal at the Kalaloch Lodge. I have fish & chips and Jenny orders chips & fish.

When we begin to look for a campsite we are surprised to see the campground almost full in this sort of weather. There are only a couple of campsites left and they are close to the road. Once again we find ourselves circling through all the campsite loops trying to decide which of the bad campsites is best.

> by the time we have
> unpacked—the inchworm
> finished scaling my tent

After setting up camp we take a leisurely walk on the beach.

> arriving with the tide
> an empty crab shell
> yet unbroken

> dead loon on the beach
> its head nods as each wave
> comes and goes

Following our walk we walked over to the Lodge for some desserts and tea. Jenny won a piece of pie in a bet earlier about whether or not we had gained elevation riding into the Hoh Rain Forest. We enjoy eating, drinking tea and coffee, and good conversation for almost two hours.

I feel I'm getting to know Jenny a little better. To my surprise I find that many of her beliefs are like my own, the only difference being that our beliefs are based in different philosophies.

Back at camp we split a bottle of "Alaska beer." Really bad beer! And we take turns rubbing the kinks out of each others' shoulders and backs.

Wednesday

Woke up earlier than usual this morning. Maybe it is the sound of the rain hitting my tent that woke me. I get dressed and go outside to see what the weather looks like. It's not really raining anymore. The rain drops that woke me were falling from the trees. When I reach a viewpoint where I can see the horizon and the beach, I can see brighter skies approaching. I head back to camp to start breakfast and packing up. By the time Jenny comes back from her walk, we can see blue skies now not too far in the distance.

As we start today's ride the sun comes out!

We really need to find a laundromat today because our clothes are very dirty. In our search we find that the Lake Qunault Resort is the only place nearby with a laundromat. So that becomes our next destination today.

Later...

Taking a hot shower and having clean clothes feels so good that we decide to stay here for the night and make a big push for Lake Nahwatzel near Matlock tomorrow.

Jenny has become preoccupied with reading the map and trying to figure out the mileage for the remaining portion of our trip. I think she is apprehensive about riding on gravel or dirt roads. We have each had a flat tire so far and to be honest I am myself a little concerned. We have two inner tubes left with no place in the area to purchase more spares. But I do not share this with Jenny. It would only reinforce her concerns and almost guarantee that the rest of our ride will be on Highway 101.

How can you have adventure when you are prepared for everything and avoid taking risks?

Jenny and I have soup for dinner and then play a game of five-in-a-row, a variation of *go*. After Jenny beats me every game we walk over to the Lake Quinault Lodge where Jenny buys me a beer, and we play a quick game of backgammon.

Back at camp we decide to go to bed early. This is hard to do because the campground is full of people who are here to race sailboats this weekend and they are in a festive mood.

The couple next door just started playing folk songs on guitar and mandolin. Now they have started singing loudly as though giving a performance or welcoming everyone to join them. I envy them for their closeness and the love they share, which is apparent in their voices as they harmonize. Listening to them sing a song together I find myself crying because it is so beautiful and also because I do not have that in my life.

> campground
> couple next door singing
> I sit crying in my tent

Thursday

I am awakened by the sound of pouring rain. I go back to sleep hoping that when I awake the rain will have stopped.

I am awakened by the sound of pouring rain. I start packing things up in my tent. The floor of my tent is soaking wet. When I go outside to take a look around I see that both of our tents are sitting in big puddles. It's amazing that we haven't floated away! I take a short walk down to the waterfront and I am surprised to find that it's not even raining. All the drops of rain on our tents are falling from the trees above. In fact as we are packing up the sun comes out. Jenny is suggesting that we ride over to the laundromat to dry our tents in their dryers. A great idea!

It worked! Great! Our tents are dry. But now it has started to rain very hard. We decide to head across the street to the resort restaurant for some breakfast while we wait it out. During breakfast the rain dies down to a drizzle. Jenny gets excited and comments that we should have been ready to take advantage of the break. But within minutes it starts pouring again.

Following breakfast we wait at our table watching the rain, waiting for another break, hoping for the sun to come out. The rain slows down. We go outside to put our helmets on. It starts pouring again! Once again we are chased inside to watch the rain.

Finally we decide to ride in the rain. Reasoning that probably as long as we are in the rain forest it will continue raining all day. It feels great to get moving. Even in the rain.

Almost as soon as we reach Highway 101 the rain starts to slow down. Within an hour or so we reach the intersection leading to the dirt gravel road through the national forest. It is a moment of decision for Jenny. I am hoping she will agree to go on this more adventurous route. She agrees!

A few minutes after starting on the road east the sun comes out. A good sign.

As we reach the end of the pavement there is a steep gravel hill before us. Jenny complains a little about the grade and the gravel but I am relieved that she hasn't mentioned turning back.

Once we start heading south towards Matlock the road becomes a gentle sloping downhill grade for most of the way.

Now and then the road becomes rougher with scattered potholes forcing us to slow down. The road is following a river valley down from the high country, occasionally opening up to reveal panoramic views of the surrounding wilderness.

every slope
the sun has touched
rising mist

The grandeur of this land once so wild is so powerful that I am forced to stop by its imposing beauty. It is in places like this that I can most easily sense the presence of God.

Crossing a bridge I am so excited to see pavement that I carelessly ride over the metal edging of the bridge. I get a flat tire. It is my rear tire so I am forced to take everything off my bike to fix it.

We have been riding underneath a patch of blue sky which now leaves us behind. It starts to rain. Jenny makes peanut butter sandwiches for a snack (I think she uses every opportunity to lighten her load by using up her two-pound jar of peanut butter). The flat is fixed within ten minutes. I am conscious of the fact that we still have many more miles of gravel road and only one spare inner tube left between us.

We finally hit pavement for good just outside Matlock. It is getting late as we pull up to the Matlock general store/post office/gas station for a snack. The woman working here tells us several logging roads just a mile or so away lead to clearings that are acceptable camping spots. She assures us that it is O.K. to camp there as the property belongs to a large logging company and everyone in the area uses their property for recreation.

Jenny and I find a clearing and make camp. It is dark and we are going to sleep right away so Jenny sleeps in my tent and doesn't bother setting hers up.

For getting a late start this morning we sure covered a lot of ground today, and most of it was on gravel roads. I read a little bit of Gandhi's autobiography before falling asleep.

Friday

Woke up fairly early and started packing up. Our plan is to eat breakfast at the Lake Nahwatzel Resort restaurant this morning. The sign on the door says closed but the door is open. I peek inside and see that their dining room is filled with customers. Later we find that the restaurant was opened earlier than normal to accommodate a logging company party. Although the restaurant is not open to the public we are allowed to have breakfast anyway after the loggers leave.

The woman who worked at the grocery store last night in Matlock also works here in the morning. We find out that she is supporting five children and that she has two jobs. We proudly show each other pictures of our kids.

If we can ride close to a hundred miles today, this will be the last day of our ride. I feel perfectly able to do it. I wonder how Jenny will feel later today.

We ride on Highway 101 north until we reach Route 108, which takes us northeasterly along the southern shores of the Hood Canal. The scenery is beautiful.

blue heron
eating its
reflection

blue heron
stalking its
self

In Union Bay, a pleasant small town about six miles down this road, we take a break for snacks and refreshments. Deck chairs have been provided on the porch and we happily take advantage of them.

Our ride along the Hood Canal takes us through many quaint small towns. As soon as the road meets up with the larger and busier roads and highways leading to Bremerton our riding is less pleasant. I can think only of reaching some of the smaller, more familiar country roads farther north near Kingston.

Near Bremerton Jenny starts to feel ill and wants to take a break. I decide to lead us into Bremerton to catch the ferry into Seattle so that we can take a shorter route Jenny suggested earlier. She becomes angry with me that I did not consult her about the decision. We decide to get some food and take a break before making a final decision.

Jenny decides to go north taking the longer, more scenic route. It's agreed then. We ride north.

We experience some difficulty with traffic and finding our way out of Bremerton but within a half hour or so we are on the open road again. I feel ready to ride two hundred miles today!

The remainder of our trip is relatively uneventful and in familiar territory.

The Black Forest

I had planned to get an early start this morning. But I find myself sleeping late. Leaving my wife and a warm bed is hard to do.

The long drive to Leavenworth is picturesque. All the trees are displaying their fall colors.

I'm waiting for breakfast at the Black Forest Restaurant in Leavenworth. It is about two o'clock and I still have about twenty miles to drive before reaching the trail head. I'm alone this trip. I couldn't find anyone else who had the time or wanted to hike sixteen miles or climb 3500 feet this weekend. I'm glad now that no one came with me because I am intent on climbing to the top before it gets dark four hours from now.

While sipping tea I fondly remember my last hiking trip out here with my friend Lisa. We hiked up to the Enchantments that time.

old steam engine
rumbles through the black forest
restaurant

The climb up is steep. It is pitch dark as I am nearing Lake Margaret. I started too late in the day. I haven't taken any breaks on the way up, as a result my legs are cramping more with every step I take.

on arrival
from across Lake Margaret
owls cry—whooo

I set up camp by candlelight.

Second day

I wake up to the sound of light rain hitting my tent.

getting water
empty pot chiming with each
rain drop

boiling water
steam escaping
the tent

The rain has slowed to a drizzle. I'm going on a hike up to Lake Mary
to see what it's like.

cradled
in a pine branch
red leaf

orange, dry
grass field
white fog

raining
dry grass
rattles

Finally reached Lake Mary after climbing two very steep miles. It has
stopped raining for now.

reflecting
dry grass meadows
Lake Mary

eating chocolate
just the way I like it—
frozen!

on every blade
of grass—water
droplets

Back at camp, I start packing up. I'm going to hike down and camp a couple of miles from the trailhead so I don't have to rush down on Sunday. Also the weather may be better lower down.

silence
a rotten branch falls—
silence

I set up camp next to Icicle River and then relax reading and writing cowboy poetry. Here's one I wrote just now:

Salami and Beer

My thighs are sore from yesterday's climbin,
And my knees are sore from today's downin,

My back's sore cause of this pack on my shoulders,
I guess I'll sit down on a boulder,
I'm out of shape, that's why I'm sore all over.

It's been rainin all day
just like I knew it would
But there's nothin I wouldn't pay
for this chance to be in the woods.

Because the weather is so bad I haven't seen a soul,
Only some white-tailed deer and some water fowl,

I wish my wife could be here,
to enjoy eatin salami and drinkin beer,
ever since we had them kids,
She can't get away to go on these trips.
Maybe when we're old and gray,
we'll start hikin and campin together again some day,
In the meantime I'll just sit and drink my beer,
And pretend my wife is near.

Looking at the trees I'm inspired to design a new sort of tent that uses a tree's trunk as its central support. I spend some time sketching my ideas in my journal.

Woke up at night to the sound of a small animal trying to get into my tent. I lit my candles and went outside to look around.

surrounding trees
in the dark—
tent's light

pine needles
falling—listening
for rain

river
rushing by—listening
for rain

in one
corner of the tent—
garbage

opening
the zip-lock—stink
of blue cheese

blowing out
four candles—the last one—
darkness

Lying in the dark, trying to fall asleep, I had a moment of enlightenment! I quickly wrote it all down in my pad…

as above
so below

Above God focuses on us. Tries to be entirely conscious of us, the
parts of the whole. Below, we focus on God. Trying to be conscious of
God the whole.

Third day

It is drizzling this morning. The two trees I camped between kept the
rain off and my tent is mostly dry.

I took the hike down to the trailhead at a leisurely pace.

dry river bed
all black stones
yellow leaves

rain begins
falling—leaves
also

I'm back at the Black Forest Restaurant and I am informed by the wait-
ress that I am having breakfast for lunch.

Far from Home

I am Leatty von Heart. I am 59 years old. And I am traveling west. Finally?

"As in you better do it before you die?" I'm not sure, but it's more than a metaphor. It's a real direction with crossroads, signs—and distance.

Space. A woman in space. Finally.

> traveling west
> all those wide open spaces
> fenced in

Does that mean that space is gone? Used up? Well, if it isn't space, it's space coupled with time. Changed into time. The time to cross a bridge. Back and forth.

(Helen—remember. Did we do it once? What did we say? What our lives were? That they were hard? That we were mountains? Yes, that we were mountains.)

Back and forth.

Slowly.

So slowly the present is always the present and the bridge is always there. Nothing more. Nothing less. Step by step. A promise.

> as I watch
> a rainbow disappears
> into the mountain

Not a pioneer.

The pot boiling. The Indians coming. The snow falling. The baby crying. The baby dying. First. And then the others. So many.

Stories.

Space squeezed into a wagon, into wagon wheels, wagon ruts. The next pass. The next bend. The next river. Time borrowed from stones and wildflowers to mark a grave. To do it right. To make it pretty. To keep it safe. The distance of a life. The telling squeezed into a letter. Gone.

A woman.

So they wouldn't be faceless.

> summer breeze—
> in the small cemetery
> flags flutter

Making the trail. Following the trail.

Going west.

Now it is Leatty von Heart going west. Traveling. Me. Without my husband. Without my children. Without their children. Without birthdays and anniversaries and holidays. Wandering outside the chain of life. Wandering on the edge of purpose and need. On the edge of loss and disconnection. An observer.

Looking.

Entering a dream and looking.

> abandoned mine—
> finding a pretty stone
> for my grandchild

Searching.

Coming. Finding. Leaving. And leaving again. Slipping into the landscape. Becoming part of the landscape. Becoming part of what I can only see but do not know.

Wilderness?

It is not for me to say.

Content to find the next meadow. The next stream. The next mountain. And content to leave them. This one. That one. One after the other. So many they become the same. So many I discover the rhythm of sameness.

a heartbeat?   far from home—
it is like a heartbeat.   one crow or another
it is like the next day.   waking me

Idiot

I did not like driving for pleasure. But I did not feel like going back to the apartment.

I did not want to engage in any human contact. So, I took a right and a left and traveled into this and that direction for a short while.

I did not want to explore the consequences of existence: I was spiritually exhausted. But I glanced at the brown rug lying on the back seat and saw one person's need. Then I saw the demise of all people: the same thing happening to the many—making us one, long before the disappearance of the one.

I made a right and a left followed by another left. I had had enough. I was hungry and probably in love and I was squandering this precious moment with metaphysical introspection.

"Drive, you idiot. It's a beautiful day, can't you see?"

> clearly winter
> through bare branches
> the sky

Zazen

Prayer can take any form.

Sandy had fallen into a dreamless sleep. I had fallen into the movements of my thoughts. Watching, letting go; drifting, straightening my back: this was the process of zazen. And this simple process of "just sitting" on a cushion in the best possible lotus position was the essence of Zen—no, a practical manifestation of the spirit (that was Zen).

My presence stopped. And with it the abstraction of time. Time. The passage of time. I shook my head and stood up.

I looked at Fish and wondered: was time an element of the personality? Did time cease with the individual?

I was the universe, wasn't I?

He was the universe, wasn't he?

Where did the universe go?

I looked at my cushion. What happened to my prayers?

> between space
> and time...
> infinity arises

Climbing Kachina Peaks

Wake at 3 A.M. and make a cup of tea. Moon through the window a waning gibbous.

> lift kettle from stove coil—
> orange glow
> lights the kitchen

Planning a hike up San Francisco Mountains, the Kachina Peaks. I throw a few things in pack: thermos of hot water, tea bags, cheese, bagels, an apple, bird book. Hop on my bike for ride to the mountain road.

> pedal along dark road
> Jupiter too
> speeds through pines

At 3:30 in the morning no car even on the busy route to the Grand Canyon. I turn off at mountain dirt road, park bike among pines away from view. As I walk, sporadic clouds obscure moon, map no longer readable. Without the moon, which way?

> car suddenly here,
> suddenly gone—
> dark mountain silence

Even in cool moonlight the road dust coats my tongue.

hike by moonlight
dead pine's
sudden jaggedness

As I climb to a pass, the gradual light of dawn emerges from the sky.
Still dark beneath the trees.

dawn light—
white flash
of junco tail feathers

leaves rustle—
among pines
pale aspen

Hike along thinking of haiku. Stop for tea at sunrise, write them down.
Forget some. Sun rises over painted desert. Distant mesas' black juts
horizon.

blue asters
closed tight—
cool dawn

sunrise
pines above me
glow orange

Pass through field full of flickers, leaping from grass to tall dead limbs.
Fifteen or twenty at least in this one spot. Secret in their throats, a wild
cackle. Farther up the trail three bull elk grazing. One astride the trail
turns to sniff the air. Considers me a full minute.

          bull elk on trail—
          glad
          he's not fierce

Not much sport in the hunt, but it will start soon anyhow. Not long
now, these might be dead. They amble off down the slope into dense
cover, huge racks gracefully avoiding branches.

          elk cross trail—
          their scent
          lingers among spruce

Didn't think to bring the field guide, and an unknown mushroom. How
many more I don't know about, alive beneath my feet?

As I move higher up the mountain, aspen begin to yellow. At first only
the top few leaves flutter golden, then leaf by leaf suffused. On ridge-
line dead bristlecone pine low to the ground. Huddle behind it out of
the wind. How long it lived here, now bone-whitened by mountain
winds. On the lee-side, sheltered from gusts, flowers manage, and a
good spot for lunch. Look across basin to tallest peaks.

          the harsh wind—
          tea in tin cup
          quickly cold

On the Kachina Peaks nature removes a mask.

          thin cloud drifts off peak
          hoarfrost glitters
          on black boulders

Where the snows come from. Soon I will be up there.

Clark's nutcrackers seem terribly wild as they fly near timberline, piercing the wind with their clattering. Several juncos bathe in trail dust. Spin in little dust piles, feathers twitching. Reluctant to leave as I approach, they return as soon as I pass.

Nearing the summit, only bristlecone pines and lichen remain to be seen of life.

> tiny bristlecone
> lichen-covered boulder
> I breathe too

Trail follows cinder-block ridge to top. Wind grows immense.

> kicked a minute ago
> boulder far below
> stops rolling

On the distant horizon, Grand Canyon north rim looms above the invisible gorge, cut deep into earth. Brilliant depths invisible from here, hidden beneath everywhere. To the east, beyond painted desert colors, remote Hopi mesas break level horizon. Their prayers, in spite of tourists and ski lodge and hikers such as me, turned towards this sacred ground. At the summit, so windy I can't stand up. Home of the kachinas. None that you'd notice though. Maybe they've gone dancing. Clouds form over these mountains, carry rain to distant fields, whether we pray for it, whether we don't. Somewhere up here, under a rock—which one none of my business, or yours—a prayer bundle. Still, good to know. Thunder sleeps in these boulders.

Turn to descend into wind. Pass many hikers on their way up. "How much farther?" "Are we almost there?" Some Sierra-clubber types who look like they'd rather be reading about it.

Walk quickly back into trees, wind eases. Juncos scatter before me, but Clark's nutcrackers high overhead don't notice. An hour later, in a meadow sheltered by aspens, I lie in the sun, drink the last of my tea, watch gold leaves shimmer in sun and breeze. Far above now, the summit. So recently I was there. From the flanks of Kachina Peaks, spruce, aspen sprout.

> suddenly here
> grasshopper on my knee
> suddenly gone

At a small spring I stop for a sip. Water right from under spruce tree root.

> glance back
> juncos return
> to the cool spring

Thinking of a shower, and hot supper, and how to write this, I hike through forest I don't notice. Now, after shower, and supper, and writing this, I think of forest I missed.

> cold moonlight
> on kachina peaks—
> if I step outside, if I don't

[Flagstaff, Arizona; 9/10/86]

Even as We Sleep

TV weatherman says cold wind and light snow—I step onto the dark porch. It's true, I see, as snow spirals down the street.

Later in bed, hear flakes flutter against the window. Beside me, new child growing within, my wife sleeps. Hand on her belly, I feel the baby stir. Even as we sleep, worlds, filled with restless energy, spin through the night.

> clouds loosen snow—
> somewhere above them
> stars still twinkle

Rain Drips from the Trees

i.

"More peaches grow in Pennsylvania than Georgia," he says, handing me three. Hitching by a fruit stand, a couple for the road and one, juicy, now.

Pennsylvania roadside—coal trucks rumble past, but don't pick me up. I'm heading through Canada to Oregon. They aren't. I'm not sure what's there, but sure what's not here.

After several rides:

Headwaters Allegheny River, Salamanca Indian reservation. Someone else camped here once, plucked berries by the river in the evening, tasted this same sweetness.

hitched all day—
pick a strawberry
under roadside weeds

ii.

As I sleep, the sound of traffic on nearby road seeps into my dream. I
wake to the morning birds before sunrise. Walk to the river to wash
yesterday's dust. Lift cool water to my face when suddenly, from
weeds, a heron bursts dismayed in feathers and water, struggles up the
air, useless legs dangling. Once up, he pulls head back, legs in,
stretches wings and glides downstream. Each flap a firm exhaling
breath. Turns round a bend and lost through the trees. Ripples on the
river slowly quiet.

Into Buffalo and mist-grey sky. Walk four miles through industrial traffic.
Boxes, cans, Bud bottles, a throw-away diaper in a bush. Queen Anne's
lace and wild yellow mustard sprout through the cinders. Then a ride.
Out at the border and my pack searched—camping gear, clothes,
food, books, laid on the counter. "Where you headed with all this stuff,
ay?" she asks. "Vancouver."

Sit in the Toronto subway with the junior executives and the secre-
taries. My pack against my knees sways with the turns. Cold beer,
salad, then walk out of town north to the woods.

a robin
sings again in the evening—
clear sky after rain

Pick up a jeep ride into dark. A school teacher, no work in south
Ontario, moving north to the bush. "You heard about the mosquitoes
up here?" she asks. "No. Why?" "Up north it gets so bad folks go

nuts—mosquito fever. Bush plane has to come in, fly them to a town, a doctor. Some don't live through." "How do the Indians cope?" I ask. "Sit patiently and smoke cigars." Talk and ride till midnight. She pulls off, red lights vanish into spruce forest. Leaves me slapping all night by the roadside with no cigars. In ears, eyes, down collar, up pant legs, the crazy buzzing and sting. Mosquitoes lift at dawn.

> dawn mist—
> mosquito-bitten face
> cools in the breeze

iii.

Slowest hitching in Canada, Sault St. Marie to Thunder Bay. At mid-morning a car pulls over, me bumpy, bloody with mosquito welts. "Spent four fucking days under the goose at Sault once," he says, "waiting for a ride. Hopped a freight."

> Drive the north shore of Superior
> All day through pines into darkness
> Fifty miles no light along the road
> So late now, no other cars
> Highway above the lake
> Full moon above the water
> Rocks glisten between black pine shadows
> Moonlight breaks on the shore

iv.

Through dawn grey the woods fade behind. Ahead the flatness of Manitoba. "I'm turning off ahead here. Going north to Thompson, 500 miles. Wanna ride along, ay?" "No, I'm heading west." Watch him drive off on the long road north. Five minutes later he fades from sight.

Hot soup, cold Molson Ale, and rain—crowded Winnipeg, big city on the fringe. Off the bus at the edge of town. I notice the few passengers watch me through the windows as I walk away in rain.

Hitching with back to the wind, a ride straight into Saskatchewan. A grain elevator always in sight, the same elevator all day, on the Trans-Canada two-lane. At last the prairie dry grass. Wet clothes in my pack from Ontario rain spread to dry in Saskatchewan night air. Shed the eastern damp.

> almost asleep
> a breeze wakes me—
> northern lights

v.

In the morning I walk through dry hills, rest in sun. Find in grass and dust: crow feathers and a crow's head. Search, no sign of coyote tracks. Black feathers brush in the dust, catch in tall grass. I stick one in my pack.

> dust clings
> to the crow's eyes—
> doesn't blink

The prairie's only the place we hurry through, but hitching and stuck, walking back and forth, crouching, standing, the same knoll on the same horizon all afternoon. The prairie at a standstill—Trans-Canada two-lane.

A lake across the road. Even in this quiet, can barely hear the gulls on the far shore. Three houses, a gas station-restaurant, grain silo by the tracks, and an old three-sided wooden shed: Morse, Saskatchewan. I eat dinner in the restaurant. A bell rings, car pulls up outside, then quiet as gas gets pumped. On the walls hang prairie primitive land-scapes. Between bites, as I chew, look at them: "Wheat Field with Crows," "The Return of the Hunters," "Mother with Child." Maybe painted by the guy outside pumping gas. $25.00 each. I could bargain down, but no room to carry. Buy a loaf of bread, rye. Think about his hands taking my money as I carry it back to the road.

Sunset and still no ride. White gulls, struck from the saturated solution of purple sky, crystallize onto the lake. The wind stops. No traffic for the last hour.

> prairie evening—
> in a roadside shed
> moonlight smells of horseshit

vi.

Finally out of Morse after sun-up, on to Medicine Hat. Along the road, dust and blackbirds scatter. Further off, beyond the traffic's wake, grasses don't move. Mid-morning I get a ride in a pick-up, a middle-aged farmer—his whole life just back and forth this road. He's picking up every hitchhiker with a loud "Hop in!" Soon there's fifteen of us crowded in the back, streaming through the warming air, shout-ing to be heard, drinking beer for breakfast. A can thrown back bounces silently down the center line. Suddenly he slows, stops, drops off fifteen hitchhikers at Gull Lake, Saskatchewan—home. Leans out the window, "See ya folks, ay," and rumbles in dust up a side road. Who'll ever get a ride? They line up every hundred feet

along the highway. I walk into town for lunch and a few cold beers in
a cool, dark tavern.

> farmers in the fields
> I'm alone at the bar—
> summer silence

Calgary at stampede time. Too broke to see the show, I hitch quickly
through. Ride in the back of another pick-up, climbing, climbing,
Calgary to Banff. The great plain's dry grass falls away.

Drive beside a rugged stream through fir tree shade. Tourists and
locals abound in big, round, fat, black inner tubes, carried up roadside
gravel and floated down the torrent.

> roar of water—
> even louder, a stellar jay
> screeches

Hike up a hill by the road to camp. Two hours after sunset, sky and forest still twilit in the far northern night. It rained here before I arrived.

> the sky clears—
> fir needles
> dry in the wind

vii.

I wake, start a small fire with fallen needles. Lean back against a tree.

> warm in my hands
> steam rises from a cup of tea—
> haze around the mountain peaks

All day hitching from Banff to Jasper, seven hours at Sunwapta Falls. Sit by the road and watch clouds, embodied one by one out of empty air, coalesce and slide beyond the ridge. Get out my stove and fire it up to make tea. Read a book. Curse at the passing Winnebagos.

Finally into Jasper after dark. Stock up on water at a gas station. Looking for a place to camp, roam the shrubs and grass in the shadows beyond the station lights. Above the tall grass a bull elk lifts his head. Rack, stretching into the trees, glimmers in the mercury light—then the crackle through underbrush. I bed down in the tall grass. As I lie awake his image hangs in the air.

> dream under stars—
> an elk's breath
> mists the darkness

viii.

Walk out to the Jasper "free camp." Set up by the town to deal with all the summer transients and unemployed hippiedom—the sort of folks who bed down in the tall grass behind the gas station. An uneasy truce between the townsfolk and the travelers. No Mounties raid the camp for drugs, nobody shoplifts in town.

A mountain lily node across the trail. I lift it aside to pass.

Walk into a summer encampment of plastic teepees, lean-tos. Flutes and guitars under the trees, under the mountains, under the stars, all night. Sit the evening around a fire with a fellow named Gamal. "I meditate here, by the river," he says, "all day sometimes. I can journey through space, my spirit that is. The rest of me just sits here. Mostly I like Jupiter. Been there many times, very colorful. Giant peaceful creatures like whales drift in the clouds."

Off through the night, around another campfire, loud screaming, drunken laughter, shouting, cursing. He gets up, takes a thin stick from the pile and wales it through the dark in their direction. Sits. This has happened before. They quiet. "I like it there, and I like it here too—here too, maybe even better." He lives in a plastic lean-to beside the Athabasca River, holds an engineering doctorate from the University of Texas.

Around the fire, yarrow stalks scattered apart, gathered together, then scattered again. More slender than the fingers that hold them. Creative and receptive…

		A separation:
Li:		The Clinging Fire
Ken:		Keeping Still, Mountain
		A gathering:
Lu:		The Wanderer

A mountain fire, hard to start but small fir twigs burn hot. Sit still, look at the stars, hear nothing.

> talk around campfire—
> cold smoke
> merges into stars

Grizzly and cougar roam the night landscape among the wild rose bushes. The mountain presses down. Smoke rises.

ix.

Decide to use the free camp as base for a few days of roaming in the high country. Hike up the twenty-mile loop trail. Hard rain all day and cool, low 40's. No rain now but water drips down from the trees. A vestige of the storm.

As I walk along the muddy trail, just ahead and filling with water—wolf tracks. A separate swirl in the print of each pad. A branch sways in the still air. I pass around a turn. Up the trail the wolf swings its head around and smoothly disappears. A glimpse, and I don't see it again. Mud-splattered gray confluence descends through the trees. Afternoon settles in the blue lupine.

The evening gathers. Once more I sit beside a fire. The center of the fire, simple. But reveals in complexity. Flame swirls from an explosion, a falling apart, away, flickering stare in gas, dust, a multitude of divergences, diversity. Then a coming together, coalescence, unity, repetition. Breath of the universe hisses in fire, stars, sand.

Rain drips. A lake gathers to the northeast and a stream flows by to the south. I'm here. Evening mist descends the slopes, glistens from the leaves and from the spruce needles. The fire hangs reflected in each drop, falls and bursts a splash of flame all night, in every direction, over and over.

> the fire smokes
> as I sleep
> the wolf exhales

x.

A few blue patches in the clouds of morning quickly cover over again. I drink a cup of tea, time to be moving soon. Wildflowers—purple, yellow—bloom all around. As I pack my tent, the clouds begin to lift above mountains of new snow across the lake. A jay dark from one tree to another.

Stop walking mid-day at Caledonia Lake. Eat lunch as two loons echo their calls across the water into the canyons. In the distance, beyond the spruce-lined shore, again the higher mountains are clearing, revealing a yet fresher settle of snow.

> Distant loon dives—
> the first ripple
> nears the shore

xi.

Climb all day to just below timberline at Signal Peak camp. Sky darkens with a storm's passage to the north. The Athabasca valleys between the base of the mountains—five miles wide. Rain slants from the clouds across the mountains to the valley floor. The river shivers with the falling water on its back. Drops fall here, but a strip of blue along the horizon and brief hope for a clearing—the rain falls harder. I move into my tent. Hiked twenty miles today: two marten, one coyote, fifteen or twenty elk, and one storm. The tent against the wind.

> firs bend in the wind—
> stones around the campfire
> don't move

xii.

In the high country, morning clouds of white far below obscure the river. Busy breakfast and details of breaking camp, stuffing sleeping bag, scrubbing pots, I forget where I am. Swing my pack on, look up to—the rediscovery of range beyond range of mountains.

Above tree-line all day, old snowdrifts from winter storms melt on the trail, trickle through granite chips. By late afternoon I prepare to descend as the rain begins. Cold water hits the rocks all around, soaks through my sleeves. Trudge through knee-deep crusted snow. Water streams across the frozen surface of rock, across ice-sheathed snow pack, across my face, down from the pass. A circle of snow-melt lake water so blue below. Above it a rainbow hangs projected against the far ridge. I stop to look, rest, still no words for it. Put some granite flakes in my pocket. The timberline we walk in language, a stuttered breath in thin air.

> no stars—
> looking out the tent
> splash of drizzle on my face

xiii.

Downward all day from the high-country rocks. Forested trail walked with a mind full of green and shadows. Between treetops cumulous drift in blue sky.

> horse tracks—
> distant clouds smell of
> mud and horseshit

I trudge back into free camp near dark.

xiv.

After a deep sleep all night, mist hisses as I eat breakfast. On mountains rain falls every day, and the mind's river fills. As I leave the free camp, in the rain, the lily nods lower across the trail. Lifting it aside a few drops fall on my hand.

Hitched out of Jasper, west and south. Friday night in Valemount. Along all highways, in pencil, in marking pen, on the backs of signs, on guardrails, poems and curses of the road, but in this place, a warning: "Don't get stuck here at night." All the traffic headed to the bars in town. Down the road, two teen-age French-Canadians, no luck hitching either. "Where to?" I ask. "Flanagan, to pick apples." All they have stuffed in two gym bags. "It's getting dark, how about I buy you guys a cup of coffee, and call it a day." "Thanks, sure." Not much talk. We drink coffee and wash up in the restroom, then move into trees back from the road. A restless sleep disturbed by rain. At first light I leave them huddled against a tree in soaked sleeping bags.

> I also will pass these two,
> left by the road
> under pines

xv.

Shaggy green Cascades, hunched asleep, Sasquatch.

Vancouver in the early evening, lights coming on. Into a bar, chaos of smoke and ale. Can't afford another, someone I don't know buys it. Not out until after 2 A.M. Now I remember, oh yes, "Unrelieved sobriety is itself an excess." Heavy pack, wander the night streets, nowhere to go. Sleep in an alley behind weeds under tall concrete. Find a park

at first light. Stretch out on a bench. Catch the morning ferry to
Nanaimo.

> ferry surges—
> in the sea wind
> slowly sober

xvi.

White houses flicker in the water as the ferry turns into the bay.
Behind the docks, a hilltop park. Walk up the narrow street. A few picnic tables on the grass, a few large stones beneath the trees.
Petroglyphs by those who've been here before chipped into the
stones: A coiled snake unwinding clockwise, beside it, another, curling
back to sleep. Beneath my hand, more recent carvings in the picnic
table. Typical latrine scrawl, a penis entering a vagina. "For a good
time..." etc.

Out in the distance warm sunlight settles on the waves. I eat a basket
of strawberries, an avocado, and a quart of buttermilk beneath blue
sunlit sky.

Hitch out past the city's spread. Camp at the island's center beneath
clear purple air. I had not expected them and the island mountains
startle me.

A cold night. I wake before dawn, needing to pee. Stand naked in the
moonlight.

> as I pee
> steam rises—
> the moonlit forest

xvii.

Anxious for the sea, no breakfast in damp early light. Two loggers take me cross-island to the coast. A cup of coffee from large silver thermos spills on the sharp turns. We disagree on clear-cutting, but bid each other honest farewell.

Pacific Rim, smooth shore curve. Light mist blows in from the sea, up the beach, into the forest. Dense, dark, silent fir and the open, light, roaring churn of the sea. On the upper beach, huge cut and seaworn logs, tossed in inextricable piles, loosed from the rivers, blown by surf here in storm to roll up beach.

Walk all day to the camp site. Many other tents but few people visible. I step up from the beach into trees. After pitching my tent, I sit facing the ocean from beneath the trees and wait for the fire to catch brightly.

High tide ebbing. A few clues to what lies out there strewn on the beach. Pick up a crab pincher that still swivels in its hinge. Put it in my pack. Sleep with the sound of the waves—nothing, all, nothing, all.

> water swirls up sand
> sifts back
> again

xviii.

Breakfast oatmeal and tea beside small fire. Then I stash gear in the tent, fill daypack with food and water, and strike north up the coast.

Around the first turn, black lava rock flows into hissing ocean foam, cold cliffs of ragged stone tear the sea. Above the roar, along cliffs by finger and toe grasp, mile after mile, the essence of cliff—hold on. I climb down the rock edge to caves worn by high tide, bottomed arm-deep in broken shells and storm-polished stone. Churned back and forth for centuries. In a handful, tiny moist stones glimmer. I fill my pockets and clamber away onto high sea-mist rock. After sitting where the cool spray rises, I turn inland, cross-country, into humid rain forest tangle. Step by step through branches, eyes full of sweat, grab root and pull. Elbows bend, reach, and grab again. Much farther than I thought. Finally, I scale a ridge to break upon clear green lake lain amidst the trees. Walk old trail out to road, back to camp by evening.

> trees drift in sea mist—
> rain
> taps on the tent

xix.

Hour beyond hour in the darkness, adrift through sleep, I hear rain, rain awash more loudly than the waves of high tide. Wake to more rain, gradually, in grey light.

At first let-up, the other campers pack tents and gone. Solitude through tenacity. Eat in my tent, read. Near noon a yellow sun spreads moist wind over the sea. Gulls walk the sand with gathered wings. I go out to them. They run, look back, then fly out to a rock island near shore.

> waves break over rock—
> gulls, spray
> fly

Steam rises from beach logs in green light. Grass stalks hung with drops twist in the breeze.

Evening after all day's rain, sky clear, nighthawks slash above the trees. After such rain a long time to get fire started. I blow on it...coals burst orange and...turn from smoke in eyes. Coals dim. I blow hard and... dizzy. Sit as fire fades again. Blow once more, and damp wood finally catches. Galaxy of embers grows.

Finished eating, sip tea, write. Sharpen my pencil with a knife. Yellow shavings on pine needles shine in the glow of the fire. As I scribble, pages dampen with dew.

I walk to the beach to scrub pots, swirl the sand around, scrape down to a metal sheen. Look up across the water, to where summer constellations, Lyra and Aquila and Cygnus, shine beyond the mist. Constant calm rhythm of the surf stretches around. Stars thrash in the beach sand, glitter, and return to dark. Above the sea, Antares, the red heart of Scorpio, lingers in the eye.

> stars through twilit haze—
> even after the sky has cleared
> rain drips from the trees

xx.

After waking, I drag sleeping bag to beach, spread wet clothes in the sun, on dry sand. Walk beach all day, sit and read, do nothing.

> dense mist—
> in dawn light a gull
> again finds land

xxi.

Once more a morning, sky clear. Thin haze slides off the sea into the trees. Small cumulous scatter over the inland mountains. I break camp and head for the road. Hitch cross-island all day. "Ever seen such windy roads as on this island?" "Sure, back in Pennsylvania, even windier." "Naw."

Victoria, buy a few peaches, toss pits into the sea. To what avail time, waiting for the ferry.

> cross the straits
> through evening blue
> venus behind thin clouds

I lean on the rail. Tonight too, crossing Victoria ferry, white sea gulls high in the air float with motionless wings. To what avail space.

In the distance the lights of Port Angeles begin to come on. A few bright stars above them.

[6/27–7/18/77]

The Goldfish Vendor

The goldfish vendor
turned the narrow lane
followed by children

—Shuran Takahashi

The moment of pure delight is an ephemeral thing. One minute it is there, and the next—like the goldfish vendor—it has disappeared around the corner.

The daily duties and responsibilities of the adult world are governed by anxiety for the future. Scheduled work cannot be interrupted. The enjoyment of pleasure must be postponed until the appropriate time. When the goldfish vendor passes by, the adults look up briefly, shrug their shoulders, and turn back to the task at hand.

But children (and poets) know that delight does not present itself by appointment. Like a cat it comes when it will and must be taken up promptly lest it escape. The glittering gold having been glimpsed, the children are reluctant to let this enchantment slip away. They follow the vendor. They do not need a goldfish; indeed, they probably have not got the money to buy a goldfish; however, the joy of looking and long-ing is often greater than the joy of possession.

This small adventure of the children also offers the possibility of drama and suspense: who will buy the goldfish, and how much will they pay? Which fish will be chosen first? And so the children, indifferent to the past, unconcerned about the future, pursue their present happiness as long and as far as possible—until all the fish are sold, or until the ven-dor travels beyond the boundaries of their neighborhood.

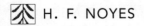 H. F. NOYES

Pines

Bashō said, to learn of the pine go to the pine. Passing along a trail by the summer sea, I glance at a big pine tree and feel I know less than nothing. Nature, like things of the mind, bears looking into. So I walk to the foot of the tree, looking up at the countless old brown cones invisible from the path. I lie down on my back and watch the movement of the boughs in the breeze. Down low, the branches are bearded with dried-out, dingy needle clusters still clinging to dead wood. Yet just a bit higher up the needles are fresh enough to bring to mind Ryota's familiar haiku:

> The pine tree—
> Ten fingers in a row:
> how green it is!

A trio of bird's nests suddenly—plain in sight—come into focus. What we see and what we miss seeing! Now the Dakota Indian teaching is clear: "When there' s nothing to see, look."

Peering up at the highest boughs, I spy those smaller, yellow-green cones fresh and shiny in the sunlight—which, I believe, most passers-by never lay eyes on. Here is spring in midsummer come to the pine, that is all year round engaged in self-renewal:

> Old stone pine
> Holding each year
> More of spring.

The tree becomes more and more like a part of me—or myself more a part of the tree. The dead and the living, I think to myself, exist side by side, and in the seasons of the mind spring can break forth anytime.

Coming back toward summer's end, I find layer upon layer—horizontal cordons—of delicate fresh green needles proudly borne by the same old pine. If I were a painter, this would be my first choice as a subject. I cannot think of anything in this world that speaks more vividly, more strikingly, of eternal spring. And when I return on a night in autumn, there's the joy of seeing what the Zen master Saigyō saw:

> The ancient pine
> Trickling all night long
> Shiny drops of moonlight.

One of the bird's nests has vanished. The other two are clearly visible against a brightening sky.

On a November afternoon, walking home through a small playground-park, I see a large old pine that reminds me of the pine at the seaside. I stand long looking up into its branches. Pigeons perch in the topmost boughs, enjoying the late autumn sun. Voices from the playing field have warned all nest-builders to keep their distance, but the pine tree seems to welcome me. I feel a kindredness:

> The old gnarled pine
> More cone brown than needle green—
> Winter soon.

Road Through the Stars: Feb. 24–27, 1994

Feb. 24, 1994

Waking in the middle of the night in my old room at my folk's place, now called the bead-room. I've thought of a title for a travel diary. Here where the towns join one another the sky is light enough to write without turning on a light or opening the curtains and so I do.

> On a chilly night
> Preparing for an endless journey
> A star through curtains.

This room where I've awakened again and again in dreams when somewhere else.

Without the inspiration of a Japanese poet of long ago I probably wouldn't be beginning this diary, something I've always previously shrunk from…which leads me to think of the combustion patterns of stars and in turn of the different ways that time may be said to have effect.

The dark, sweet fragrance of the elms is comforting, restful.

Feb. 26

Rain dripping from the firs onto the roof of another house. Staying at a seldom-occupied place in the most thinly populated section of the coast of California. Two months ago, on learning of a job in Japan starting in April, I decided that there was no point in maintaining my own household if my half-brother and his woman friend would let me spend my last couple of months in this country at an unoccupied place they own. About one third of the time I'm visiting in suburbia, the rest here.

Twenty-five years of writing sorted out, thank goodness for a woodstove. Probably better for me not to trouble with the vast disparity I see between the mainstream media of this country and the actual state of matters.

For many years I've thought of Japan, one of the names for which is "Land of the Gods," as being sort of a metaphor for heaven, especially culturally. Although of course in relation to there, nature on this continent seems like heaven...

And it seems that an open integration of the sides of this planet that science has been denying will be a natural part of the process that will lead to recognition and exploration of star travel. Will we harness the demons in our sun or simply teleport, or both? The issue of "mind over matter" does indeed imply a compassion which is ever expanding and never self-satisfied. The dominant techno-culture has heard that Machiavelli forgot to include magic and faith in his calculations, and is discovering that evil destroys itself.

> Not learning from its mistake
> Chewing on my soap again—
> A big mouse.

Feb. 27

> Wild creature scraping
> The corner of a window
> —Lonely winter night.

Loneliness is not a matter of solitude, but of juxtaposition. An old house far from the neighbors or a phone, with the rain and wind being some of the friendlier visitors, and none are invited in.

A way station where, limiting my expenditures, I get ready for a spring move across the biggest body of water on the planet.

Technology has upset the natural balance of things by pretending to ignore the most mysterious sides of our world. Consequently it's getting shaky and what has been denied and oppressed gets more of an edge. The peak of the planet is naturally the messiest and most vulnerable in such matters. Movement through a large arc seems certain to be a help in my case.

> Rainbows of beyond
> Burning within and without
> Light of any kind.

The earlier part of what I wrote today was written after waking, in the couple of hours after midnight—now it's evening. Following my afternoon studies of Japanese, having seen no one, spoken to no one, written to no one all day long—I decided to refresh myself by having a close look at the river. Though I had arrived here more than forty-eight hours ago I had still not walked the hundred meters or so to the river. The river cannot be seen from inside the house. When the rains have been heavy, it's a river, otherwise it's a large stream, though called a river usually. No otters but eels mating and other fish also mating near them. Returning uphill I continued past the house and visited quietly with the herd of deer that favor this part of this meadow (because the soil's richer). They seem to be aware that I won't be staying here long; some grazed, some didn't—as I stood about ten meters from them.

> Fish mate in the stream—
> The holidays are over
> And deer stand so still.

 ANTHONY J. PUPELLO

St. Mark's Place

A crisp fall day. I am sitting on a stoop in St. Mark's Place, a section of the East Village in Lower Manhattan

> St. Mark's Place—
> a cyclist goes down
> a one-way street

known for its progressive thought, politics, art, and music—a mixture of artists, musicians, clubs, colleges, college students, and shops, especially bookstores. Energy.

> changing leaves:
> the gay couple strolls
> hand in hand

Yet, there is another side to this neighborhood.

> the old ale house—
> click-click of high heels
> across wooden floors

Known also as Little Ukraine or St. George's, it has been a bastion of nationalist Ukrainian sentiment since long before I was born.

In Eastern Europe, these are exciting yet turbulent times. In
this little village, the shops, the closeness, the ethnic festivals
are all manifestations of an earlier, more golden time.

I have a friend who was born and raised on 7th Street. He
attended a prestigious university but still speaks with an
accent so thick you'd think he'd arrived "off the boat" just yesterday.

late
October
the
way
the
wind
shifts

What do the changes in Eastern Europe mean to him, to the other
Ukrainian exiles who've been waiting for the day when they might
return to a free homeland? Is their homeland now *free*? What do they
do now? Do they drop everything, pack up and go back? What are
they thinking, what are their children thinking, and feeling, about
home?

> the far lights of home—
> linden leaves scattered
> after the storm

This building has been the focal point of their living. It has helped
hold them together, given them spiritual sustenance and strength,
molded the character of their children. What will happen to this institution, center of their cultural and social lives, center of their children's educational lives? Ten, twenty or thirty years from now? What
will happen to this institution tomorrow, now that the *enemy* no
longer exists?

And still…

> passing clouds—
> St. George's cupola
> darkens, lightens

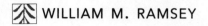 **WILLIAM M. RAMSEY**

Gurdjieff, Zen, and Meher Baba

1. Desert

> the wind numbs:
> my fingers slowly grasp
> the coffin handle

of my infant's little box, lighter than a shovelful of soggy dirt this early December dusk, yet heavier than a pile of laundered diapers. The hearse door clicks behind us. Soon we climb a short, snow-sodden rise to the sheltered spot, where despite the canvas canopy

> the grave is puddled:
> the priest thumbs his bible,
> and i twist my lip

much as a vine encircling a pine creases the trunk it chokes. Then i'm shaking like a worm impaled by the hook, twitching in spastic, jerking arcs. Later—after just a while of agony—they lead us off, my wife cold and dazed, like a deer that mutely licks the toothed steel clamping its hoof, while

> the body lies stiff
> among clods—a felled tree
> in a highway cut

or a dead rat in a culvert's mouth. The hem of the priest's robe now is spattered with mud. The softened turf sucks my shoes each time they rise, and when they fall the muck sucks them more; i think, in distracted shock,

no more of this:
hymnbooks, votives, vestments,
latin so dead

so irrelevant to how his heart valves, quite unceremoniously, fluttered
partly open, partly closed; and irrelevant to his brown irises glinting, in
blank hospital silence, like rosary beads left scattered in a salt desert.

2. Sea

Rising from the blanket and my napping wife, i walk far up the beach
unknowing exactly what i feel today, until a falling blur of whiteness
over the water tells me:

the gull dives in,
lifting to heaven
an angry fish

3. Garden

Shirtless, i feel the sun warming my back as i pull a few weeds, pinch
tomato suckers, hoe the corn rows, and feel with blank vacant satisfac-
tion fatigue creeping into me, displacing thought. Soon i go to the
cool dark of the shed, and i linger there, inhaling air made sweetly
boggy from the open, half-used bale of peat. Later, emerging with the
pitchfork, eyes lowered from the day's glare, i stroll toward the compost bins, pausing briefly when a movement in the grass catches my
eye:

a beetle eating
what is left—glinting
copper green on dung

and i smile knowing that nothing on earth, not even waste, is waste, and all is somehow incredibly rare, and i will tell this to my wife if she is strong today. Minutes later, bent at work in one of the bins

> turning compost,
> my smile twitches at a toad
> speared on the fork

4. Rice

The moisture rising in the bamboo steamer swells each grain to full-ness. It's rice never tossed at bride and groom; but when it softly meets my tongue it will marry my returning desire. Peeking under the lid, i also see the broccoli flowerets glisten, their stalks exuding juices. The peeled carrots gather beads of wetness; the onions are almost clear. Lately, i have lost my old desire for meat. Indeed, today i shud-dered driving past

> A stiff raccoon
> praying for his error
> by the roadside

as at the farmers' market earlier, standing near the country hams, i felt agitated, then depressed. But in this dusk, in this nightly rite of urgent flesh and yet more hungry spirit, our hearts find solace in broccoli, car-rots, onions—and in one level cup of rice, poured in precise and need-ed measure. Then, over tea, we talk of Gurdjieff, Zen, and Meher Baba—pretending to assume, once again, that life is sweet as well as rare. Later, at midnight,

> her hair smell
> in my face, my fingers
> count her vertebrae

Prayer for the Soul of a Mare

1. Lizard

In the quickly chilling twilight, on a log in the backyard woodpile, where I've come again to split seasoned oak into kindling for the evening fire, a lizard halts. Frozen by surprise it stares stiffly, its skin brown as the scale of bark it grips with tiny, sure toepads.

In its eyes surely i'm immense, shadowy, an uncouth god whose silhouette steals now the moon and stars from heaven, and who reaches for the axe with dark intent. From my stance above it, the lizard seems forsaken, a small, redundant, local quirk of protoplasm. Pausing momentarily, i almost clap my hands—as if to demonstrate that gods are only gods and cannot care.

But i now recall last winter's storm and how unnerved i was, the house cold, the pipes frozen a second day, and nobody had visited in a week. In the bare oaks the squirrels' nests were tatters as i walked quickly to the outhouse, the wind cutting me. When i stepped into the pine box, i choked. The only warmth in that frigid waste i soon released, while shuddering in a cold pissing spasm. There, for one morbid moment, my skin terribly taut, i died. February is inhuman, i groaned, thinking of what i saw the week before:

> the mare in a field,
> her bones scattered, shining
> white in the moonlight

2. Cat

Just once i stared wisdom in the face; i caressed it in my trembling hand.

My cat, dying of kidney failure, curled up for hours on the frayed towels we set in the dark bathroom corner, her nausea the last mean tug of flesh binding her to this life.

Often, as my shaking hand softly passed along her loosened skin folds, i marveled at her final spurning of offered food and water, of the sleek brown field mouse, of the deep meadow of crickets and thrushes—all vanities of her voracious youth—and marveled even more at her calm unconcern, at her feline undismay at acute distress.

Staring at that canny, half-opened eye, which seemed to know at last what wisdom is, i thought i had it. Yet as my wife rattled dishes at the kitchen sink, muffling her desolate choking, i knew that i too would never gravitate to calm detachment, to the emptiness of Zen.

Later, my puzzled two-year-old approached, announcing, "Mommy is sad," and i snatched her up, whirling like a dervish, giggling. When we tumbled on her dolls i knew that joy, like grief, unbalances me— that i could not dance for long in Sufi ecstasy.

Yes, i know we call our kind *homo sapiens* because we're wise, or nearly so. Yet as this slippery century nears its end, after some joy, and sharper pain—all i've learned is this:

> i wobble, neither
> emptied self nor drunken heart,
> in riptide currents

3. Scarecrow

Walking on Harrel's farm in a windy afternoon, in the torn cornfield stubble the shadow of my self is strange. It has no ideas. It is mute, never moaning, but never laughing.

Wind rushes through it.

Untied to flesh, it depends on flesh. Obscured in dark, it depends on light. It doesn't flinch at my hurled clods, or my surly kicks. Yet it flees when i chase it. As yet i haven't found it social:

> my soul's so vacant—
> no solid, stick-ribbed thing
> of flap and straw

 BRUCE ROSS

Aglow

For some time now the late November days have been bleak. Once or twice there have been moments of brightening. To cheer myself I had gone last night to see *The Secret Garden* and recalled Keats' "magic casements" for some reason, enchanted as I was with memories of when as a child my father took me to see the animated version of *Alice in Wonderland*. We had walked in after the film had begun. It was one of my first trips to the movies. What I remember is entering a sacred special place. The dark theater demanding a sense of awe. And there at the end of the tunnel of darkness the magical animated figures in brilliant pastel colors—a figuration from another dimension. Of dream. Of spirit. And the breathless rising shots last night in *The Secret Garden* of a diminishing wild landscape covered with the moving of shadows of clouds in bright light.

So I jogged my ritual run this morning in Durand Eastman Park in the drizzle:

> November drizzle—
> the squirrel's head beneath
> the wet leaves

and drove back home in the, now, light rain:

> November rain—
> the outdoor jack-o'-lantern
> collapsing on itself

In the afternoon I went to a bookstore for the signing of my anthology *Haiku Moment*. The sales were fair but I had a good time (the manager said that she would have no trouble selling the remaining copies during the holiday season). On the way home on the expressway my attention suddenly was drawn to a haze of flame at the horizon. The late afternoon light was collected in the top of the stand of naked trees on the horizon. I was somehow transported to some other dimension. I remembered the smile I had when I left *The Secret Garden* last night. I was, in some intangible way, home:

> late afternoon light—
> the stand of bare trees aglow
> on the horizon

Winter Moon

I had a very late dinner of vegetable tempura at the Plum House. The sky was shiny black with bright stars which I wanted to look at before I went home. Then I somehow forgot what I wanted. I drove home rather than spending time looking at the stars. As I parked my car I noticed that the sky was completely covered with rolling gray cloud masses and a huge shimmering moon low on the horizon was emerging. I looked at it trying to remember something.

> late winter night—
> out of dense gray rolling clouds
> the shimmering moon

Winter Haibun

The crisp, predawn air buoys me across a field shimmering with rime. Just inside the edge of the woods I sit on a mouldering log. Nearby, a sapling leans toward the first saffron stains of the new day. It is torn and scraped. When the sap rises it will die.

Night slowly comes apart, dissolves into pools of purple. Lavender washes the mottled bark of near pines.

They begin as a whisper out across the crown of the forest. Now they hum a lullaby, now mimic a far-off freight. They toy with my senses, rise, fall, undulate along uncharted paths. They search to my left, now to my right. The scattered elements gather, intensify, relinquish all their secrets. The train rushes full at me.

> midwinter—
> dawn winds approach
> the buck's rubbing tree

Water Spider

Casting my eyes down through the clear water of the shallow brook to its boulder-laden bottom, they wander in a cool trance, tracing sunlit green stones and the silent underwater curl of moss, until they are baited by the rhythmic foray of a mysterious meandering light and shadow formation, five submerged tiny pods gliding over stones, each pod a shadow enclosed by a diffused halo of light; five ephemeral pods closing together to become one and then opening and closing again and again, motions in time tracing breath's flow over bony ribs; tracing briefly the crucifix, the magic discovery of *homo ad circulum's* head, hands and feet, and then the snow-angel wonder of youth, arms pumping its wings to exhaustion, then finally fully extended these magic pods become our gliding five-point star; while all the while above us, somewhere, floats the draughtsman, silent and unseen, of such natural art; and all the while we too continue to float in many dimensions, never really knowing the in and out of our protozoic roots.

Tracing the brook stones
Shadow of water spider's
Many dimensions

A Mosquito Net on Tobago

Arriving late in the evening at the furnished cottage on Tobago. The mosquito net—does it not somehow subtly transmute the phenomena that pass through it?—visual, auditory—even the tactile sensation of a breeze felt within the net has a finer nature or quality to it.

> Moonlight,
>   wind and bamboo:
>   the mosquito net

> Midnight rain
>   on the sheet iron roof:
>   the mosquito net

> Piping frogs
>   in the silence after rain:
>   the mosquito net

In his *Journal* Thoreau remarks, "Frogs are the birds of the night."

The steep path winding down through hillside brush to a charming cove flanked by jumbles of black basalt rocks jutting into the ocean. The narrow crescent of sand less than a hundred yards in length. The waves breaking against the rocks in fountains of lacy white spray.

The small, crescent beach—
  belly-surfing on the crest
    of a great ninth wave

Mid-day nap;
  a sea breeze
    ripples the mosquito net

Renting a motorscooter for exploring the island. To the farther end
where a hurricane struck a few years ago.

The side of the hill,—
  six or seven wooden steps
    leading into air

Mountaintop trees
  blasted by the hurricane;
    the sky's tropic clouds

Bamboo—my favorite tropical tree (though botanically an arbores-
cent, or woody grass). Groves of it frequently.

Mountain-side pause,—
  the stems of tall bamboo
    creaking in the wind

The old cemetery on the road between the cottage and
Scarborough, the capital.

A tethered cow
  among the leaning tombstones,—
    the breadfruit tree

Buying local produce among the stalls of the outdoor market.
Doing a little sleuthing and convincing myself that generally I am
being charged the same prices that local people pay, but sometimes having to haggle a bit or simply shaking my head and walking
away.

> Outdoor market stall
> -but she paused a bit too long
> when asked the price

> Saturday market:
> a live hen in the scale tray
> -my tomatoes next

To the cove for a bit of sunning and swimming (or "bath" as the
islanders call it).

> Scurrying crabs
> on the spray-wet basalt rocks
> …a copper penny

And just as I delight in finding a penny, so do I enjoy building
sand castles.

> The path from the cove,—
> a childish castle of sand
> for the rising tide

To the historic town of Plymouth on the other side of the island.
Old cannons of Fort James pointing out to sea on top of the cliff.
Goats and cows cropping the grass around the ruins.

Copying the famous, cryptic inscription on a tombstone here.

> *Within these Walls are Deposited the*
> *Bodies of Mrs. Betty Stiven*
> *and her child. She was the beloved*
> *Wife of Aley B. Stiven*
> *to the end of his days will deplore*
> *her Death which happened upon*
> *the 25th day of Nov. 1783*
> *in the 23rd Year of her Age*
> *what was*
> *remarkable*
> *of her*
> *She was a Mother without knowing it*
> *and a Wife without letting her Husband*
> *know it, except by her kind indulgences to him.*

To the cove late at night.

> Coconut palms
> rustling in the midnight wind,—
> the moon-sharpened waves

Returning to the cottage.

> Sweeping beam
> of the harbor lighthouse:
> the mosquito net

An old man cutting brush and weeds with a cutlass in the cemetery.

> Cutting graveyard brush
> -picking the tombstone he needs
> for whetting the blade

A slight movement along the edge of the road attracts my eye—dime- and nickel-size pieces of something green in motion,—a moving line of pieces of green leaves being carried flat side up, each piece by a single ant.

> Tropic sun
> on the nape of my neck,—
> the parasol ants

Mid-afternoon, to the cove.

> The cove's driftwood log,
> bleached and weathered silver-gray
> ...the blue butterfly

Dawn—and a mocking bird (called "day clean" by the islanders) sings a brief tune. Another mockingbird repeats the notes; then the nearer one sings another tune. If the other bird does not answer or does not accurately repeat the notes, the first mockingbird repeats that particular tune until the other bird sings it back correctly.

> Early morning light;
> a day clean in the mango
> ringing the changes

Reading the poems of John Clare this late afternoon and early evening. Noticing on the local library's date due slip in the book that this library is one place that inflation has not entered: "A fine of ONE PENNY will be charged for each week or portion of a week the book is kept over the time."

> The deep whistle
> of a departing ship:
> the mosquito net

The sea offshore from the cove—marvelous for snorkeling.

Snorkeling offshore,—
    canyon after green canyon
        of curious fish

Fascinating, the man-o'-war or magnificent frigate bird soaring hour after hour without a beat of its wings—yet the black color and backward slanted ends of its close-feathered, widespread wings remind me of replicas of membrane-winged pterodactyls swooping down on some other creature of the Mesozoic Era. In fact, the frigate bird feeds mainly by forcing gulls and terns in flight to disgorge their own catch of fish and then snatches this food in mid-air.

Black frigate bird
    out of the age of reptiles;—
        the shore's basalt rocks

Waking at night:
    the sound of the surf
        through the mosquito net

Last day at the cove
    -a little snowman of sand
        left facing the sea

 DAVE SUTTER

Italia: Quattrocento / Ventecento

Summer, 1991. *En vacances* in Italy: Milan, Liguria, Cinque Terre,
Tuscany, Umbria, the lake district—the shoulder, hip and spine of this
diminutive giant of a country. More than other regions in Europe, Italy
to me is the quintessence of contrasts and extremes—in geography,
culture, history, and psychology. It hasn't changed since Dante—except
for technology, it is the same divine comedy, a manic mix of "shit and
shine," the sacred and profane…Michelangelo and Mussolini flip sides
of the same coin. The Vatican, for example, houses the world's most
penitential religion in a palace more opulent than Versailles, with beg-
gars squatting at its door…

> In the piazza
> a blind man trying to sell
> broken statuettes
>   (Rome)

The vast stretches of time—Etruscan, Greek, and Roman ruins;
medieval, Renaissance, and modern cities—set the mind on edge: it is
too much to grasp at a glimpse, or in a lifetime. The density of history,
the layers of time and events—the Medicis and the popes, Venice,
Florence, and Rome, each vying, in Shakespeare's phrase, "to bestride
the world," to bring heaven and hell under rule and make a profit at
the same time—weigh on the mind and agitate the soul. The sense of
"time past" and "time present" is insistent and pervasive, tangible as
the weather…

Two farmhouses:
twenty feet apart,
800 years apart
(Tuscany)

The hilltowns in central Italy span the centuries. In Monteriggioni, a
perfectly preserved medieval village, its protective walls fully intact, TV
antennas sprout on the slate roofs above turbocharged Fiats parked in
the town square. Monteriggioni is a quiet place; the few faces one
sees are mute, as if antiquity and the deep amber glow of the summer
hills had stilled the mind as well as the tongue...

Many footsteps echo
in the empty streets
of the ancient towns
(Umbria)

Family life, social life, sex, and almost everything else in Italy revolves
around the dining table—the *ristorante*, the *trattoria*, even the noisy
pizzerias. Food is the catalyst and currency of Italian culture and society. At a modest *ristorante* in Siena, the *antipasti* stretched the length
of an entire wall...

Everywhere,
even in the hills—
the clatter of dishes
(Tuscany)

The broad flat plain at Pisa accentuates the horizontal and the vertical,
like a de Chirico painting. Arriving at noon on a sunny day, the planar
effect is heightened. Near the foot of the famous tower, I sit in the

shade of a cypress, eating a pomegranate, while the sounds of school-buses and children, miraculously speaking Italian, swirl in the warm summer air. Milling and laughing, running and shouting, making the most of their day away from the classroom...

> schoolchildren
> leaning to look
> at the tower
> > (Pisa)

A few miles south of Florence, in a wooded valley, there is an American military cemetery. A neoclassic memorial sits on a slope a few hundred yards from the entrance. Stretching to the left and the right are the graves, marked by the typical regimented rows of small white headstones receding into the distance. A small visitor center adjoins the entrance. There is no other car in the parking lot. The architecture, landscaping, and the sunny wooded setting are idyllic and serene, as if the men there had never gone to war. In the graves registry in the visitor center, I find the name of an uncle I never knew. There is not a word to be said, and no one to say it to...

> American cemetery:
> myself, a stray dog,
> the only visitors
> > (Florence)

At last Florence, quintessential city of the Renaissance...

At street level the noise of the traffic is deafening, a cacophonous roar of underpowered, overgeared vehicles, all designed to maneuver the complex maze of narrow streets and congested squares at maximum speed and decibel levels. Step off a curb without looking six ways at once, and back again, and you're dead!

The grime of centuries is embedded in the pores of the city, in the crevices and interstices of its stone walls and facades, its monumental architecture and heroic public art, all stained and sullied by time and the emissions of countless internal combustion engines...

> Rising still
> above the city's squalor,
> Brunelleschi's dome
> (Florence)

At the Uffizi, the Palazzo Vecchio, the Accademia, the cathedral with its magnificent dome, the Medici palaces and gardens, one can achieve a degree of sanctuary, of peace and repose amid the perfection and timeless mastery of Quattrocento art. Donatello, Leonardo, Michelangelo, Raphael, Caravaggio, Bellini, Mantegna, Botticelli... The masterpieces march from wall to wall.

Botticelli's female faces—*La Primavera*, *Venus*—immortalize the purity of innocence, yet there is also in these images, as in *Mona Lisa*, a knowing glance, an inward smile, a secret sense of self and purpose impenetrable to men. I had seen that selfsame smile a week before on the lips of a topless Italian beauty on a beach on the Mediterranean...

> Botticelli venus
> sunning herself
> on the Riviera
> (Liguria)

The culminating experience for an art lover in Florence is perhaps the statue of David at the Accademia. A week before a demented artist stubbed its toe with a hammer, I stood and watched the statue for hours. It moved and spoke eloquently. In the perfection of the piece there is more than mere mastery of technique; the statue comes to life as a coda of grace in action, tension in repose; it is possibly the purist expression of the classical theme of man mastering brute nature, subduing the inchoate forces of the universe.

For centuries the statue has stood as it stands today, in a state of perfect poise, of exquisite balance and control, ready at an instant to kill or be killed...

> The statue of David:
> so tense, so calm—
> stone made flesh
> (Florence)

Reaching for the Rain

1

Just born—
the cry of a stranger
in the spring stillness

Tony Suraci

Rarely, amidst the happiness that parents experience at the birth of a child, do they stop to consider that a stranger has been born to them. What the child will be like they have no way of knowing. Not only is he a stranger to them but he's also a stranger to the world, a stranger in a strange land.

For the first time
tiny hands
reach for the rain

Ross Figgins

2

Spring breeze in the park.
On the stone unicorn's back
a child flies away

Ann Atwood

The spring breeze, wafting over the new flowers, the new leaves, is full of magic, inspiration. The little child breathing its fragrance is easily affected by its intoxicating power. And in a flight that only a child can take, he gallops across the heavens.

> In the greening park
> the children and vendors...
> first balloon going up
>
> *Jaye Giammarino*

3

> An ogre perhaps?
> Old school building swallowing
> long lines of children.
>
> *Lorraine Ellis Harr*

Wordsworth has said that delight and liberty are the simple creed of childhood. But the fun and freedom that children enjoy are severely curtailed by the strictures of school. Until finally, for the great majority, regimentation becomes accepted as the order of the day.

> In sudden silence,
> children at crossroads line up
> to board the school bus.
>
> *Anne Landauer*

4

Wind
    tugging a kite
        tugging a boy...

            Bonnie May Malody

Perhaps the great charm of kite flying is that you feel the kite as an extension of your being; you feel as if your spirit were soaring into the sky. An exhilarating experience—and one that can be enjoyed alone or in the company of others.

        the wind—
            full of laughter
            and kite strings

                Ross Figgins

5

Out in the backyard
    my child enjoys the music
        of a squeaky swing.

            Marilyn Bolchunos

A mother pauses at her housework as she hears the music of the squeaky swing. The sound tells her that her son is enjoying himself, as he always has in the backyard. She remembers...how much fun he's had digging holes and making tunnels, building forts and climbing trees. And although he's outgrown most of those pleasures, still, on occasion, the old swing entices him.

> Boys in sleeping bags
> feel the different backyard
> that lives in the night.

> *Kay Davis*

6

> For the circus clown
> summer is the long season
> of his painted smile.

> *Adele Wirtz*

It seems that children of all ages love the circus and especially delight in clowns. The daring of lion-tamers, acrobats, and tightrope walkers keeps children on the edge of their seats, but clowns give them the gift of laughter. Yet beneath the painted smile sometimes we can detect an underlying sadness.

> Lo, the circus dwarf
> once again contemplating
> his lengthy shadow...

> *Emily Romano*

Watching stars come out
   one by one in the pale dusk
      his toy forgotten.

Madeline Beattie

In this haiku we see the natural wonder to which childhood is heir. But as the boy grows and matures, will he keep his inheritance or will he squander it like a prodigal son? Will he become so enamored of the world and its affairs that he'll lose his primal sense of wonder?

Dusk darkens to night—
   voices from the playground
      drift into silence.

Lorraine Ellis Harr

Sunset on Cadillac Mountain

July 28, 1992

I crouch near the summit of Cadillac Mountain, awaiting sunset. A driving wind cools the bald granite. Sparse clumps of flowering meadowsweet and daisy, springing from shallow seams in the rock, sway and bob in the gusts. Below, numerous freshwater island lakes, long and narrow, run parallel to Somes Sound, making Mount Desert Island a patchwork of land and water; beyond, humped islands rise in the bays, extending the crazy quilt pattern for as far as the eye can see.

The sun—huge, sagging, and red—appears in the distant haze to flatten under its weight and settle onto the knobs and ridges of the pink and blue mountains of the western horizon. Surveying the patchwork of waters, I find each segment mirrors the pastel sky: Eagle Lake and Somes Sound, centered before me, shine pink to reddish bronze; to the north, Western Bay and the Mount Desert Narrows reflect slate grey; and Blue Hill Bay, to the south, glows with burnished amber. The colors change constantly, a kaleidoscope of land, sea, and sky.

As the sun drops below the horizon, the lakes and bays brighten in startling relief against the sky and mountains; soon, the waters radiate a lambent silver, as if poured molten from a ladle. Jupiter sparkles on the southwest horizon, and the black islands begin to glitter with lights—tremulous and yellow, they shimmer along the shorelines and dot the dark, forested island interiors.

Under a gunmetal blue sky filling with stars, I am alone in the encroaching darkness, the only sound that of gusting wind.

yarrow in the path
aromatic sharpness
penetrates the night

The Temple of the Snail

March 8, 1993

In bright, afternoon sunlight, I arrive at the Temple of the Snail. Energized by an approaching rainstorm, I scramble to the top of a thirty-foot dune sheltering the temple. To the east, the turquoise sea swells with rising wind under threatening clouds that move steadily toward land. Yellow pollen, swirling from the white blossoms of honey flower, sweetens the sea air. Mockingbirds flit in and around the succulent bushes, their calls punctuating the ocean's steady roar.

clouds of gnats
swallows swoop and dart
feeding noiselessly

Shielded by the belly of the dune, the ancient temple stands beside an old Mayan roadway at the edge of a brackish mangrove swamp stretching to the western horizon. Relentless wind bends the mangrove trees forward and sweeps across the lagoons. Momentarily, the stacca- to clatter of mangrove leaves dominates even the sound of the sea. In the shallow lagoons, fluttering white heron wade and spear the glittering black water, throwing their heads to the sky as they swallow prey.

A curtain of rain forms over the ocean and moves toward shore. When the first drops crater the sand, I dash for shelter in the old temple, startling a large Sawyer lizard lounging on a stone shelf that mantles the temple door. As racing clouds obscure the sun, I crawl into the temple's cramped outer chamber and squat on a large rock. My view cropped by the small stone doorway, I watch blades of zebra grass dip and snap from ground to sky, shedding the falling water. Now and again, propelled by driving rain, the orange bell flowers of a primavera tree skitter across the temple entrance.

> sharp windgust
> hard rain softens the rattle
> of chit-palm fronds

In this ancient sanctuary, the urgency of primal vision radiates from the stones. Sheltered by such venerable antiquity in our evanescent world, I echo Wordsworth's plea:

> ...perish what may,
> Let this one temple last,
> ...devoted to eternity!

> (*The Prelude, VI* 433–35)

In perhaps half an hour, the mesmerizing storm recedes and soft drizzle surrounds the temple.

Abruptly, a scraping noise vibrates from the inner sanctuary. Startled, I grope through the narrow arch and peer into the inner room, where a colony of hermit crabs pours from a crevice in the sunken stone floor.

Each drags a gaily colored seashell across the ancient hewn stones, tapping its red claws forward to test the rubble before struggling across it. In the dim light and mossy dampness, crabs claim the temple where oracles spoke.

Now chilled by the dank rock and rising moisture, I crawl over broken stones and squeeze through the temple opening, rising stiffly under a diffused gray sky. In the stillness, my fingertips trace the raised fossils texturing the temple's weathering stonework. On the temple roof, small nettles, rooted between stones, droop under the weight of clinging water.

> murmuring sea
> a blackbird's liquid call
> slurs across soft air

Early Morning

Thankful I didn't die during the night, I get up at dawn and wander out into the yard. The air is fresh and cool with just a hint of fall. After a sweltering summer it's like a promise that has been kept.

> Pale dawn,
> beyond the rim of night,
> spreads across the sky.

In our town the suburban streets are quiet and deserted at this hour. It's as though they stretched on and on to some dim infinity. From time to time a night bird will worry the stillness with tired little notes.

> Unheard—
> roots tightening
> their grip around stones.

Across the way my neighbor's screen door slams, and a small white spaniel bounds into the yard. He scampers about, here and there, trying out space, barking at silence. He, too, seems glad to have made it through the night.

> First light of day—
> what ghosts of night remain
> blend into shadows.

The Circus

country road
a circus-poster tiger
in the spring rain

The circus in Dover, New Hampshire, where we moved when I began the fourth grade, was always in a huge field across the road from Gages Farm. It usually came to town toward the end of summer, but the posters appeared long before the circus.

I would get up early the day it was to arrive and go down to the field along with other local boys. We'd try to get a job helping out as we watched the circus people put up the tents. "Hey Mister, can I help do that?" You might help pull out the folds of a tent while it was still on the ground, or pull on the ropes to raise it, or be sent to water the animals, or be asked to carry things from one place to another. Once I was even allowed to help pound the stakes for the ropes holding up the tents. For our work we'd get a ticket to the Big Top.

from the tent
a clown looks out
at a scarecrow

I especially remember the grass. It was a marvel to me the way the circus grew out of that grassy field. The tents would go up and inside and outside there were fields of grass. But under the muted light that came glowing through the canvas the inside field had a strange enchantment about it.

a morning breeze blows under the circus tent

The grass soon got pushed and matted down from all the activity, especially at the entrances, but in one corner of a sideshow tent you might still see a daisy nodding. Or just beyond the fat woman's tent a couple of thistles would show blue against the bottom of the giant canvas banner that pictured her several times life-size.

a canvas sign
billows in the wind
"The Fat Lady"

rising over
the freak-show tent
a gibbous moon

Carrying water to the elephants, camels, and other animals made me feel I'd been brought into contact with distant places around the world—places in Africa and Asia. The smells and sounds as well as the look of these animals brought a new sense of the earth into my life: its variety and novelty seemed endless.

straw
on the elephant's back
summer breeze

holding his Stetson
the circus cowboy wipes his brow
with the back of his sleeve

The circus often had a Wild West show. This was the part I liked best. Perhaps some of the acrobats doubled as cowboys, or even Indians, but they all seemed real to me—a world apart from the clowns and lion tamers. As the Indians dashed into the arena in pursuit of a stagecoach, throwing up dust from a New England field that had turned into a western prairie, they were in turn chased by a group of galloping cowboys, and the "Wild West" was here—now—right in front of me.

> during the Wild West show
> the setting sun lights the posts
> of the empty corral

The main show in the Big Top always started with the grand parade. All the people and animals of the circus entered, decked out in elaborate costumes with great plumes and blazing colors. The elephants, horses, camels, lions, tigers, dogs, clowns, and all the performers marched around the inside of the tent and out again and then the ringmaster came out alone in the spotlight and with a fanfare the circus performances began.

> the ringmaster enters
> all the horns of the band
> point skyward

When the same thing was happening in all three rings under the Big Top a magical feeling of mirroring or recreating swung the mind with wonder. Our eyes would go from one circle to the other mesmerized by beautiful trick horses going around and around in each one. There would be slight variations in these duplications and in the man or woman with their long stick-like whips in the center of each circle, but these only added to the magic spell. The center circle might be made up of all white horses. In the outer circles, they might be all black in one and all brown in the other. These trim and graceful creatures would in unison change from trotting to galloping to walking to prancing to rearing up. They would all at once, on cue, swing about and circle in the opposite direction. Their heads would all nod in rhythm with their pace. They had colorful cockades sticking up from their foreheads that nodded also.

Then would come the bareback riders in every ring. Each dazzling princess in tights rode standing on the back of a circling horse. Then she would stand on her hands and do acrobatics on top of the horse as it ran around and around, head bobbing to the sound of the circus band. Then the high wire acts. Then the trapeze artists. Then the lion tamers. And all the time the clowns running and falling and flapping and playing tricks on each other.

Then there would be a grand finale with a man being shot from a cannon or a tightrope star performing the most daring feat ever attempted on the high wire. It seemed like it could go on forever. But then it was all over and the wonderful color and noise were gone and there was only a big crowd moving out of the tent, leaving behind a disarray of soda cups and flattened popcorn boxes.

> standing on one foot
> the bareback rider rides her horse
> into my dreams

Curbstones

A cool warm March wind blows off the East River and along a side street near New York City's South Street Seaport. The morning sun is coming out again after a spell of grayness. The light flows up the street, shines on the curbstone at my feet, flickers faint shadows along its irregular surface, and suddenly awakens within me the realization that I am once again in love.

Each spring I fall in love with granite curbstones. These natural-looking rough-cut stones with their slightly rippled surfaces, their precise and monolithic solidities lining and defining a street from here to infinity, have for me the mysterious presence of mountains, the strange, halted stillness of great glacial deposits: at once stopped and journeying—waiting millennia, yet instantaneously moving through space with their star, our star.

Some granite curbstones have smooth tops—not polished, but simply flat as if planed. These have an artificial look and sunlight is washed out on them. On the more common, rough-hewn curbstone the light is varied and soaks the stone with its magic, playing with shadows and intensities. On rainy days small pools form here and there along its top while the gutter stream flows below. The stone is closer to nature—wild and alive.

> waterfront bar
> the cobblestones glow
> in the night rain

I grew up among the granite landscapes and seascapes of Maine and New Hampshire. From the mountains of New Hampshire and from rocky, mist-shrouded islands off the Maine coast have come the foundation stones of many of our towns and cities—for buildings and bridges, for statues and memorials, for cobblestones and curbstones.

Still seen on little streets near the Boston and New York waterfronts are granite cobblestones, many of which were quarried from Maine islands. There is a stillness about them on chilly, rainy days in spring or autumn that suggests such origins. Wet and streaming like the rocky islands they were carved from, they call up a vision of the Atlantic splashing up against lonely shores, the sun coming out to shine on great, wet rocks gleaming amidst the desolate reaches of the rolling sea. For a hundred or more years these cobblestones have been dusted and smeared with the grime of the city and washed again and again with sunlight and rain. Worn smooth like pebbles on a shore, they still have an unevenness that endears them to me.

Curbstones, with much of their mass hidden in the earth below the pavement, rise above the street and show the way. Though still beneath our feet, they can be guideposts to where and how we direct our steps. Witnessing with a calm impassivity our rushing about from here to there, they also stand as monuments to the peace and wisdom that come from being still.

> fallen leaves
> the wind uncovers
> a granite curbstone

When I was a boy, curbstones were just right for sitting on, for looking at the passing of people, cars, and the passing of the day itself, or for just gazing off into space. On rainy days I would use them as banks from which to launch popsicle-stick ships into the streams that flowed along the gutters. Adventure-bound, these boats often disappeared between the iron bars of a drain, riding upon great waterfalling waves into the darkness, to continue their voyages beneath the earth.

After the run-off of spring rain, streaks of sandy dirt were often left behind in the gutters. Made up mostly of sand spread on the streets during the winter, these deposits sometimes took the wavy, rippled shape of the waters that had washed them into the gutter and that had flowed over and around them. As I would sit dreaming on a curbstone it was pleasant to shuffle my sneakered feet in this sand, making little designs with it and feeling its softness against the hardness of the pavement. Putting my hands down by my sides I could also feel the curbstone—the cool, smooth roughness, the solid reality of the world holding me. In the afternoon I would watch the stone's shadow move slowly from the curb's edge into the street along with my own. The sun-warmed sand would slowly cool in the shade and I would realize it was time to go home...before going, I pick up a handful of sand and hold it in the fading sunlight, then let it run through my fingers back into the shadows.

I am still drawn to granite curbstones, and in all seasons of the year—in the heat of the summer, in the coolness of the autumn rain, or in the cold winds of winter—but I am always surprised by the love I feel for them on the first sunny day in spring.

> morning sunlight
> under the Brooklyn Bridge
> a curbstone shadow

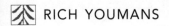

For My Wife on Our First Anniversary

Early spring. I wake to pale light, to the dogwood outside our bed-room window, a few cruciform petals barely visible. My wife lies there beside me under flowered sheets: one thigh touching mine, her brown hair fountaining against the pillow. In half dream, she murmurs—a low sound, distant yet familiar. This is our life together. Slowly, the sky brightens; sunlight washes our room, breaks through window prisms into tiny rainbows. I search them out as if on an Easter egg hunt: one on the frame of the standing mirror; another on my chest of drawers, under the photos of us laughing and hugging. And others—on my nightstand, the cedar chest, the Japanese lantern hanging over our bed.... My wife stirs, turns toward me. A rainbow appears on her cheek. Soon she will wake, our day will begin. But for now we lie here, content, her breath warm on my skin. I kiss her cheek...

> prisms in
> early light:
> we make love

Sunday Visits

I never knew my grandfather when his words were clear as spring water and spiked with a brogue strong as Irish whiskey: the man with the lilting tenor, who sang rebel ballads as he carried the day's mail; who argued daily with the corner grocer over the price of pears, then overpaid with a flip "Keep the change"; who at weddings sang out toasts with the abandon of a child, and over pints at O'Fenn's wove boyhood tales of Ireland—of nights spent in the sweet smell of peat fires, when his own grandfather would recount the heroics of Wolfe Tone, Emmet, Pearse, and Collins.

I knew him only after his second stroke, his lilt gone, his left leg strapped to a brace. By that time he had moved in with my aunt and spent most of his hours in the living room, on a sofa the color of weak tea, staring into the fireplace. We visited every Sunday evening. Always, my parents followed my aunt into the kitchen to help with dinner, leaving me on the sofa with my grandfather. He would speak to me, sounding as if he were underwater—the gargled syllables of a drowning man, incomprehensible. Occasionally an understood word or phrase bubbled through—"How's school?"—from which I wove whole conversations about my teacher's unkempt beard and my attempts at long division and Friday's hot lunch and anything else I could think of. But usually I couldn't understand a thing, and simply nodded and agreed: the last refuge of the baffled.

I think he saw through me, though, for sometimes he would abruptly laugh and slap my knee; I, of course, would laugh with him. And other times he would look away into the fireplace, at pale brick blackened by soot, and say nothing at all…

twilight…
shadows seep into
grandfather's quiet

Bibliography

Periodicals

Albatross: Magazine of the Constanza Haiku Society, Romania

Frogpond: Journal of the Haiku Society of America

Modern Haiku

Point Judith Light

Books

Ashbery, John. *Haibun*. Columbes, France: Collectif Generation, 1990.

Bashō, Matsuo. *The Narrow Road to the Deep North and Other Travel Sketches*; Nobuyuki Yuasa, tr. Baltimore: Penguin, 1966.

Bostok, Janice. *Silver Path of Moon: Haibun*. Mt. Gravath, Australia: Post Pressed, 1996.

Easter, Charles. *Spirit Dances*. Flemington, N.J.: Black Bough, 1997.

Evans, Judson. "Haibun for Dennis: December 12, 1994," in *Hands Full of Stars*. Boston: Aether, 1995.

Harter, Penny. *At the Zendō*. Santa Fe, N.M.: From Here Press, 1993.

Herold, Christopher. *Voices of Stone*. Redwood City, Calif.: Kanshiketsu Press, 1995.

Higginson, William J., and Penny Harter. *Met on the Road: A Transcontinental Haiku Journey*. Foster City, Calif.: Press Here, 1993.

Issa, Kobayashi. *The Year of My Life: A Translation of Issa's* Oraga Haru; Nobuyuki Yuasa, tr. Berkeley: Univ. of California Press, 1960.

Japanese Poetic Diaries; Earl Miner, ed. and tr. Berkeley: Univ. of California Press, 1969.

Kacian, Jim. *Six Directions: Haiku of the Local Ecology.* Albuquerque, N.M.: Las Alameda Press, 1997.

Kerouac, Jack. *Desolation Angels.* New York: Bantam, 1965.

Little, Geraldine Clinton. *Separation—Seasons in Space: A Western Haibun.* West Lafayette, Ind.: Sparrow Press, 1979.

Lliteras, D. S. *Half Hidden by Twilight.* Norfolk, Va.: Hampton Roads, 1994.

———. *In the Heart of Things.* Norfolk, Va.: Hampton Roads, 1992.

———. *Into the Ashes.* Norfolk, Va.: Hampton Roads, 1993.

Lynch, Tom. *Rain Drips from the Trees: Haibun along the Trans-Canadian Highway.* Las Cruces, N.M.: n.p., 1992.

The Modern Japanese Prose Poem: An Anthology of Six Poets; Dennis Keene, tr. Princeton, N.J.: Princeton Univ. Press, 1980.

Neubauer, Patricia. *Foxes in the Garden and Other Prose Pieces.* Allentown, Pa.: n.p., 1993.

The Prose Poem: An International Anthology; Michael Benedikt, ed. New York: Dell, 1976.

Ramsey, William M. "Driving to Myrtle Beach," in *Modern Haiku* XXVII:1 (Winter–Spring 1996), pp. 30–32.

Roth, Hal. *Behind the Fireflies.* Glen Burnie, Md.: Wind Chimes, 1982.

Shelley, Pat. *The Rice Papers.* Saratoga, Calif.: Saratoga Trunk, 1992.

Snyder, Gary. *Earth House Hold.* New York: New Directions, 1969.

Spiess, Robert. *Five Caribbean Haibun.* Madison, Wisc.: Wells, 1972.

Sturmer, Richard von. *A Network of Dissolving Threads.* Auckland, N.Z.: Auckland Univ. Press, 1991.

Tripi, Vincent. *Haiku Pond: A trace of the trail…and Thoreau.* San Francisco: Vide, 1987.

van den Heuvel, Cor. *A Boy's Seasons,* in *Modern Haiku* XXIV:3 (Fall 1993), pp. 75–84; XXV:1 (Winter–Spring 1994), pp. 32–43; and XXV:2 (Summer 1994), pp. 33–45.

Willmot, Rod. *Ribs of Dragonfly.* Windsor, Ontario: Black Moss, 1984.

Permissions

The following abbreviations have been used:

A	*Albatross*
BS	*Brussels Sprout*
F	*Frogpond*
MH	*Modern Haiku*
PJL	*Point Judith Light*
RNH	*Raw Nervz Haiku*
u.p.	unpublished

Clausen, Tom: "Before School," *PJL* 2:3 (1993), 12; "Birds," u.p.; "New Sneakers," *BS* XI:3 (1994), 24; by permission of the author.

Dubois, Jean: "The Near and Far," *MH* XXI:2 (1990), 32–33; by permission of the author.

Easter, Charles H.: "Turtle," *F* XVIII:3 (1995), 35; by permission of the author.

Evans, Judson: "Haibun for Dennis: December 12, 1994," *Hands Full of Stars* (Boston: Aether, 1995), 27; "The Red," u.p.; by permission of the author.

Frank, Patrick: "Return to Springfield: Urban Haibun," *PJL* 2:3 (1993), 12–13; by permission of the author.

Harter, Penny: "At Home," *At the Zendō* (Santa Fe, N.M.: From Here Press, 1993), 29–30; "A Weekend at Dai Bosatsu Zendō," *At the Zendō*, 15–26; by permission of the author.

Kacian, Jim: "Bright All," *Six Directions: Haiku of the Local Ecology* (Albuquerque, N.M.: La Alameda Press, 1997), 85–86; "The Order of Stars," *Six Directions: Haiku of the Local Ecology*, 47–48; by permission of the author.

Kalkbrenner, Dennis: "Lake Superior," *MH* XXIV:1 (1993), 56; by permission of the author.

Kenny, Adele: "Only a Stranger," u.p.; by permission of the author.

Ketchek, Michael: "Chaco Canyon Haibun," *MH* XXVI:2 (1995), 41; by permission of the author.

Klacsanzky, George: "Arriving with the Tide," *A Haiku Poet's Travels in the Great Northwest*, u.p., l06–15; "The Black Forest," *A Haiku Poet's Travels in the Great Northwest*, 33–39; by permission of the author.

Lifshitz, Leatrice: "Far from Home," *MH* XXIV:1 (1993), 60–61; by permission of the author.

Lliteras, D.S.: "Idiot," *Half Hidden by Twilight* (Norfolk, Va.: Hampton Roads, 1994), 147; "Zazen," *Half Hidden by Twilight*, 140; by permission of the author.

Lynch, Tom: "Climbing Kachina Peaks," *Rain Drips from the Trees: Haibun along the Trans-Canadian Highway* (733 N Raymond Street, Las Cruces, NM 88005; 1992), 27–32; "Even as We Sleep," u.p.; "Rain Drips from the Trees," *Rain Drips from the Trees*, l–26; by permission of the author.

Neubauer, Patricia: "The Goldfish Vendor," *MH* XXIV:2 (1993), 89; by permission of the author.

Noyes, H.F.: "Pines," *A* III:1 & 2 (1994), 136–37; by permission of the author.

Partridge, Brent: "Road Through the Stars: Feb. 24–27, 1994," *Road Through the Stars*, u.p., 1–3; by permission of the author.

Pupello, Anthony J.: "St. Mark's Place," *RNH* 1:2 (1994), 35; by permission of the author.

Ramsey, William M.: "Gurdjieff, Zen, and Meher Baba," *MH* XXV:3 (1994), 37–39; "Prayer for the Soul of a Mare," *MH* XXVI:1 (1995), 34–35; by permission of the author.

Ross, Bruce: "Aglow," *MH* XXV:2 (1994), 46; "Winter Moon," u.p.; by permission of the author.

Roth, Hal: "Winter Haibun," *MH* XXIII:2 (1992), 57; by permission of the author.

Simser, G.R.: "Water Spider," *MH* XXV:1 (1994), 48; by permission of the author.

Spiess, Robert: "A Mosquito Net on Tobago," *Five Caribbean Haibun* (Madison, Wisc.: Wells, 1972), 49–55; by permission of the author.

Sutter, Dave: "Italia: Quattrocento/Ventecento," *F* XVI:1 (1993), 41–44; by permission of the author.

Tico, Tom: "Reaching for the Rain," *F* XV:1 (1992), 37–39; by permission of the author.

Trammell, J.P.: "Sunset on Cadillac Mountain," *MH* XXIV:1 (1993), 59; "The Temple of the Snail," *MH* XXV:1 (1994), 45–46; by permission of the author.

Trotman, Frank: "Early Morning," *BS* IX:3 (1992), 31; by permission of the author.

van den Heuvel, Cor: "The Circus," *A Boy's Seasons*, *MH* XXV:1 (1994), 40–43; "Curbstones," *MH* XXIII:2 (1992), 58–59; by permission of the author.

Youmans, Rich: "For My Wife on Our First Anniversary," *BS* XI:3 (1994), 15; "Sunday Visits," *F* XVII:3 (1994), 26; by permission of the author.

Index of Poets

Numbers in **boldface** type indicate anthology selections.

Amann, Eric, 15

Bashō, Matsuo, 11, 14, 28, 32, 48
Baudelaire, Charles-Pierre, 75
Better, Cathy Drinkwater, 55
Blake, William, 59
Bradford, William, 16
Bryant, William Cullen, 76

Chong Sun Kim, 75
Chuang-tzu, 30
Clausen, Tom, 64–67, **87–90**

Donegan, Patricia, 45
Dubois, Jean, **91–92**

Easter, Charles H., **93–94**
Edwards, Jonathan, 16
Eliot, T. S., 14
Emerson, Ralph Waldo, 14, 29, 76
Evans, Judson, **95–96**

Fenn, Liz, 32, 54–55

Figgins, Ross, 59
Frank, Patrick, 15, 54, **97–99**
Franklin, Benjamin, 16

Ginsberg, Allen, 14
Gurga, Lee, 45

Hackett, James W., 46
Harter, Penny, 40–47, **100–10**
Herold, Christopher, 53–54
Higginson, William J., 40–47
Hryciuk, Marshall, 74

Issa, Kobayashi, 15

Kacian, Jim, 11, **111–15**
Kalkbrenner, Dennis, 30, **116**
Kenny, Adele, **117–19**
Kerouac, Jack, 11, 14, 19–21, 60, 73
Ketchek, Michael, **120**
Klacsanzky, George, **121–37**

Lifshitz, Leatrice, 34–35, **138–40**
Little, Geraldine, 21–22

Lliteras, D. S., **141–42**
Louvière, Matthew, 60
Lynch, Tom, 11, 36–40, **143–64**

Malody, Bonnie May, 59
Moore, Marianne, 46
Muir, John, 16

Neubauer, Patricia, 56, 59–61,
    165
Noyes, H. F., **166–67**

Partridge, Brent, 47–51, **168–71**
Pound, Ezra, 14
Pupello, Anthony J., **172–73**

Ramsey, William M., 11, 70–73,
    174–79
Reichhold, Jane, 56
Rexroth, Kenneth, 14, 16
Ross, Bruce, 67–68, **180–81**
Roth, Hal, 22, 30, **182**

Saigyō, 16
Shiki, Masaoka, 14–15, 19,
    57–58
Shikibu, Marasaki, 19
Simser, G. R., 31–32, **183**

Snyder, Gary, 11, 14, 16–19
Sōgi, 16
Soseki, Natsume, 19, 73
Spiess, Robert, 32–33, 35–36,
    51, **184–89**
Sutter, Dave, 33, **190–94**

Takahashi, Shuran, 59
Thoreau, Henry David, 13, 14,
    16, 25–29, 48, 77–78
Tico, Tom, 56–59, **195–99**
Trammell, J. P., 30–31, 33–34,
    200–203
Tripi, Vincent, 25–29
Trotman, Frank, 51–52, **204**

Ueda, Makoto, 18–19

van den Heuvel, Cor, 52–53,
    61–63, **205–11**

Whitman, Walt, 14, 16, 39, 73
Willmot, Rod, 22–25
Wordsworth, William, 33, 73

Youmans, Rich, 55–56, 69–70,
    212–13

For a complete catalog call or write to:

Charles E. Tuttle Co., Inc.
Airport Industrial Park
RR1 Box 231-5
North Clarendon, VT 05759

1 (802) 773-8930